Burgess Sport Teaching Series

TEACHING TENNIS

Rick Chavez
Lois Smith Nieder

Colorado State University

Burgess Publishing Company
Minneapolis, Minnesota

Consulting editor: Robert D. Clayton
Editorial: Wayne Schotanus, Nancy Crochiere, Anne Heller
Copy editor: Gail Duke
Art coordinator: Melinda Berndt
Composition: Loni Hansen
Cover design: Adelaide Trettel
Illustrations: Lois Smith Nieder, Nicholas Hyduke

©1982 by Burgess Publishing Company
Printed in the United States of America
Library of Congress Catalog Card Number 81-71259
ISBN 0-8087-4803-3

Burgess Publishing Company
7108 Ohms Lane
Minneapolis, Minnesota 55435

J I H G F E D C B A

Contents

Acknowledgments

We would like to express our appreciation to Dr. Robert Clayton for his encouragement and suggestions, which helped make this book possible. We also wish to thank the following contributors: David Dietemann, still photographer; Reini Reiter, subject for motion picture photography; Roger Durant, Kristi McCutchen, Jeff Nieder, and Judy Nieder, subjects for still photography.

1

Introduction

Teaching Tennis is designed to help tennis instructors and coaches work with beginners, intermediate players, and advanced players. The information can be beneficial to tennis teachers regardless of their location, whether in clubs, public schools, colleges or universities, or recreation departments.

Departments preparing physical education majors can find the material useful in skill classes as well as in teaching tennis techniques courses. Instructors in such departments usually emphasize the establishment of teaching objectives, which is covered in Chapter 2.

Tennis instructors are often involved in the planning of tennis facility construction and/or renovation. Information concerning tennis facilities and equipment is featured in Chapter 3.

Class organization is an important part of teaching small and large groups. Chapter 4 covers outdoor as well as indoor instruction. Various instructional techniques are discussed in detail.

In any comprehensive tennis program you can expect to find instruction for beginners, intermediates, and advanced players. These three ability levels are covered in Chapters 5, 6, and 7. Each chapter emphasizes the appropriate strokes suggested for the specific ability groups. Teaching progressions, drills, common errors and corrections for various strokes, and 20-day teaching plans for each ability level make up the format for these three chapters.

Chapter 8 contains tennis strategies for beginners, intermediates, and advanced players. Various strategies are suggested for singles as well as doubles play.

Tennis teachers in junior and senior high schools, as well as in universities, usually need to evaluate their students' abilities and progress. Chapter 9 contains suggestions for evaluating the various strokes at the three ability levels. Cognitive exam areas and stroke analysis are also mentioned.

Many tennis teachers also have the responsibility of coaching a competitive tennis team. Chapter 10 covers the many responsibilities of tennis team coaches. Included are such areas as team tryouts and selection, schedules, contracts, budget, grading, travel, conditioning activities, drills, and a suggested daily practice schedule.

Basic tennis rules and scoring, useful for class handouts, are given in Appendix I, while the official United States Tennis Association Rules of Tennis are contained in Appendix II. The glossary of tennis terms is arranged alphabetically within the categories of scoring, types of shots, parts of the court, rules, strategy, and miscellaneous.

Suggested class/student projects are found at the end of each chapter. The projects will provide students with additional experiences to enhance their knowledge of teaching and coaching tennis.

2

Teaching Objectives

In order to evaluate the success of a unit of instruction, the teacher must establish a set of learning objectives. A *specific* statement of the learner's expected achievements is called a performance, or behavioral, objective. Simply stated, such an objective describes what a successful learner will be able to do at the end of a unit or course of study.

BEHAVIORAL OBJECTIVES: CRITERIA

To write a behavioral objective you must state:

1. *WHO IS DOING IT*
   The student

2. *WHAT HE IS DOING (exact performance)*
   Will execute a forehand ground stroke

3. *IMPORTANT CONDITIONS (if any)*
   Past the opponent's service line

4. *HOW PERFORMANCE IS MEASURED (acceptable performance)*
   Ten out of fifteen trials

The three criteria (what the student is doing; important conditions under which the student will perform; and how you will measure the performance) help make your objective more specific. To make your intent even more clear, use explicit performance words, such as: *to identify, to list, to perform, to analyze, to demonstrate, to execute.* Words open to more than one interpretation (*to understand, to appreciate, to enjoy, to be capable of*) should be avoided.

Both unit and daily behavioral objectives should be specific. Unit objectives may be stated in an all-inclusive manner, however. For example: "The student will be able to execute the basic tennis skills—forehand and backhand ground strokes, forehand and backhand volley, and the serve—and score 70 percent or better in a performance skill test on each." When all the skills are grouped together in this fashion, the teacher will state the criteria for each skill being tested in the daily objectives for the practice skill test day and the actual test day.

2

BEHAVIORAL OBJECTIVES: TAXONOMY

Behavioral objectives should cover the areas of learning involved in skill performance. A list of many possible educational objectives has been compiled in the *Taxonomy of Educational Objectives*. The taxonomy classifies educational objectives into three domains:

1. The cognitive domain, in which intellectual outcomes are emphasized. Behavioral objectives in this domain will include application, analysis, synthesis, and evaluation. Examples in tennis would include knowledge of rules, strategies of singles and doubles play, and stroke strategies.

2. The affective domain, in which appreciations and values are stressed. Objectives will deal with student interests, attitudes, and feelings. Examples in tennis are learning to accept line decisions and unforced errors in a courteous manner.

3. The psychomotor domain, in which the development of motor skills, including gross bodily movement and finely coordinated movements, is emphasized. Examples related to tennis include developing skill in forehand and backhand ground strokes, volley, and serve.

SAMPLE BEHAVIORAL OBJECTIVES

While appropriate objectives will vary for each situation, examples (which could be adjusted to apply to beginning, intermediate, and advanced levels) are shown.

COGNITIVE OBJECTIVES

By the end of the unit the student will:

1. Know the rules and the terminology of tennis, as presented in this class, and score 70 percent or better on a written examination in each.

2. Demonstrate knowledge of singles and doubles strategy by scoring 70 percent or better on a written exam which involves diagramming movements and listing responsibilities of players.

3. Demonstrate knowledge of singles and doubles strategy by using strategies presented in class tournaments observed by peers and the instructor.

4. Know and explain orally to the instructor how to select a racquet for personal use, based on standards for grip size, racquet weight, balance point, and string tension presented in the class.

5. Be able to recognize, analyze, and correct stroking errors presented in class and score 70 percent or better on a practical analysis test given by the instructor.

PSYCHOMOTOR OBJECTIVES

By the end of the unit the student will:

1. Execute these basic tennis skills: forehand and backhand ground strokes, forehand and backhand

volley, and the serve, in such a manner that 70 percent or better is scored on a performance skill test on each skill (see Chapter 9, p. 94).

2. Be able to judge ball flight consistently and position him/herself correctly in relation to the ball bounce in practice and in game play, as observed by the instructor.

3. Use acceptable form on all strokes and score "fair" or better on each, as determined by instructor rating (see Chapter 9, p. 106).

AFFECTIVE OBJECTIVES

By the end of the unit the student will:

1. Demonstrate good sportsmanship by voluntarily thanking and/or congratulating opponents at the end of the match in class tournaments and general play, as observed by the instructor.

2. Demonstrate leadership by physically and verbally aiding and encouraging classmates in skill drills during practice and leisure time, as observed by the instructor.

3. Demonstrate self-control by maintaining composure in highly competitive match play, as observed by opponents and spectators.

4. Demonstrate responsibility by seeing that school tennis equipment used by him/her is properly racked and stored at the end of each class period.

SUGGESTED CLASS/STUDENT PROJECTS

1. Construct a set of behavioral objectives for a beginning, intermediate, or advanced tennis class, to include at least two objectives from each of the educational domains.

2. Interview a tennis teacher and determine realistic behavioral objectives for beginners or intermediate or advanced players.

Facilities and Equipment

Most tennis instruction takes place on tennis courts that have been constructed by professional court builders. Tennis instructors should become familiar with information concerning the development of tennis facilities, because occasionally they are asked to arrange for new tennis courts to be built or for existing courts to be resurfaced. If this happens, instructors must familiarize themselves with the latest innovations in tennis court construction and refinishing.

FACILITIES

Most tennis courts properly constructed for school and recreation areas are built to accommodate singles and doubles play. Fig. 3.1 illustrates the official dimensions of a tennis court.

Surfaces

When outdoor tennis courts are to be built, the weather and finances will dictate what type of surface will be chosen. Hard-surface courts are more common in the northern and western states, while soft-surface courts are found more often in the southern states.

Hard-surface courts (cement, asphalt, and composition) are favored by many tennis teachers and players because they usually give consistent bounces and provide firm footing. Some dislike those hard surfaces because the balls bounce more quickly off the surface, thus making it a faster game. Hard-surface courts will also produce more low balls to hit. Maintenance on hard-surface courts consists of periodic sweeping and washing. Hard-surface courts usually require resurfacing every seven to nine years, depending on weather and amount of play.

Many players prefer soft-surface courts, such as clay courts, because such surfaces will give them more high bounces, allowing them more time to get to and stroke the ball. These surfaces call for a slower game than do hard-surfaced courts. Clay allows foot sliding and is considered easier on the legs, but the sliding also brings forth surface markings, which cause some balls to take bad bounces. Maintenance of clay courts is more time-consuming than maintenance of hard-surfaced courts, as clay must be watered, rolled, and brushed, as required by the amount of play.

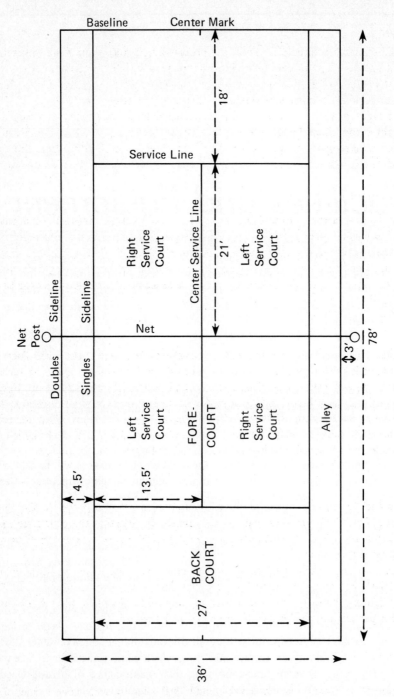

Figure 3.1
Court diagram and dimensions

Posts and Nets

A solid, stable concrete foundation for the net posts will help keep them from tilting inward from the stress placed on them by the net cables. Most net posts will have a reel-and-ratchet net tightener, and the model that does not expose any part of the turning device is recommended, as this will allow only the instructors and maintenance personnel to adjust the net height.

Most nets are made of nylon, cotton, or polyethylene materials and are sold at various prices. It is better to purchase good durable nets made of any of the three materials. Nets that are not weather-proofed will need replacement or repair more readily. In parts of the country where snow remains on the courts most of the winter months, the nets should be removed at the end of the fall season.

Fences and Windscreens

It is desirable to have a fence around the tennis courts, to prevent problems from arising due to blowing debris, animals, bicycles, wagons, and other hindrances that are not of benefit to the tennis facility. Good quality chain-link materials and posts should be installed for durability's sake.

Windscreens are considered essential by most tennis instructors because they help moderate the winds that can have an effect on the ball. They also serve as a consistent color backdrop that makes it easier to see the ball.

Rebound Walls

Rebound walls, if strategically placed, will be beneficial to a tennis program. They should be positioned so that balls mishit by players practicing cannot roll onto the playing courts. If possible, for maximum use, the walls should be placed so that balls can be hit from both sides. Fig. 3.2 shows where two rebound walls can be positioned for maximum use on single- and double-row courts.

Lines should be painted on the walls to depict net height. This will allow those practicing to see how high they hit their shots in relation to net height. Other markings can also be added to the wall so that intermediate and advanced players can hit their shots toward specific areas.

Lights

Lights are installed on tennis courts for the sole purpose of allowing people to play at night. The number of footcandles of illumination will be determined by whether the courts are intended for recreation or tournament play. Professional light installers will advise prospective clients about the lighting that will meet their needs.

School boards and city councils might jointly consider the installation of lights on the school courts in order that they might be used by the entire community over a 24-hour period. Another selling point for lighting tennis courts is that such lighting helps illuminate the school grounds, thus making it safer for participants in other night programs at the school.

EQUIPMENT

Tennis equipment is usually purchased by individual players with advice from their tennis instructor or friends. However, physical education teachers and coaches are sometimes responsible for purchasing large amounts of essential equipment for their tennis classes and teams, such as nets,

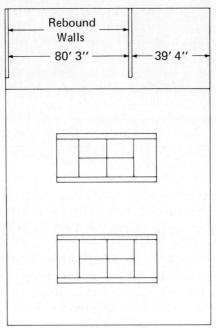

Figure 3.2A
Single-row courts

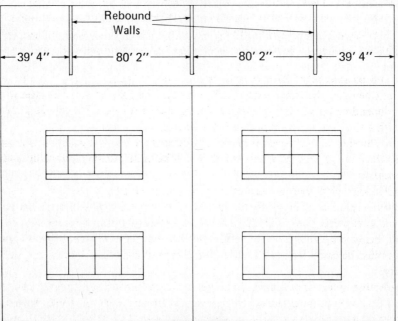

Figure 3.2B
Double-row courts

Figure 3.2
Rebound walls positioned to give approximate court depth

tennis racquets, and balls. Other items that are not essential but can be helpful are racquet racks, ball-throwing machines, and storage baskets (such as Ball Hoppers).

Racquets

Tennis racquets can be bought in different weights, sizes, lengths, and shapes, and at various prices. They can be made of wood, wood composite, metal, fiberglass composite, and graphite composite. Perhaps the best way to select a racquet is to swing several, using forehand, backhand, and overhand strokes, and then buy the one that feels best and is within the appropriate price range. Sometimes the pro or store manager will even let a person play with a demonstration racquet. Tips that can be offered to students on specific racquet components follow.

Grip size and racquet weight. "Grip size" refers to the circumference of the racquet grip, which will vary by eighth-inch intervals. Correct grip size has been chosen when the hand feels comfortable around the grip and the tip of the thumb reaches the first joint of the second finger.

Most tennis racquets weigh between 12 and 14 ounces. Youngsters and adults who do not have much strength usually prefer using lighter racquets. Players who enjoy playing at the net often feel that light- and medium-weight racquets are easier to handle. Many baseline players feel that they get more power and better rhythm by using medium-heavy and heavy racquets.

The racquet has an identifying label on the handle just above the grip, giving the grip size and weight. A racquet listed as 4½L will have a grip circumference of 4½ inches and be lightweight (approximately 12 ounces.).

The touring pros are very particular about the grip size and weight of their racquets, as their performance is largely dependent upon how they use them. An amateur should not necessarily copy the pros, since that size and weight may not suit his/her game. Students can compare their racquet grip size and weight preferences with those of the following professionals: Billie Jean King—4½ inches and 13¾ ounces; Jimmy Connors—4⅝ inches and 13¾ ounces; Bjorn Borg—4½ inches and 14½ ounces.

Length and balance point. Most tennis racquets are 27 inches in length, with the accurate (true) balance point being at the exact center (13½ inches). The balance point changes in one direction or the other, depending on whether players prefer light or heavy racquet head weight. It is believed that racquets with a true balance point are easier to control.

Stiffness. Another of the considerations in purchasing a tennis racquet is its stiffness. For players who do not hit hard, a racquet with flexibility will be better. Strong, powerful hitters usually prefer a stiffer racquet.

Strings. Persons who purchase an unstrung racquet must decide what kind of string to have put in their racquets—nylon, gut, or synthetic gut. Most recreational players prefer nylon strings because they are not as expensive as gut and in many cases—especially in damp areas—will outlast gut. On the other hand, many tournament players prefer gut because they feel that it gives them better control. Gut strings must be cared for well, as water and dampness can cause them to snap sooner than if they are kept dry.

After selecting nylon or gut strings, a decision must be made as to string tension. The tightness (or tension) of the strings is measured in pounds per square inch. A good string tension for most beginners would be approximately 50 pounds, because the ball stays on the strings longer when they are loosely strung. Nontournament players would probably have their racquet strings at 55 pounds, while first-class players might prefer 65 pounds or tighter. Oversized racquets are strung at between 70 and 80 pounds. In all cases, check the manufacturer's suggested stringing tension.

Racquet size. In recent years, the size of the racquet face has been a point of controversy. Standard racquets have a hitting surface of approximately 70 square inches, while the various Prince models vary between 85 and 130 square inches. This provides for a bigger sweet spot, the claim being that the Prince racquet has a sweet spot four times larger than the standard racquet. More tournaments are being won by players using the Prince than ever before, and some coaches feel that it is the racquet of the future.

A midsize (middie) racquet has also been developed. The middies are about 20 percent larger than the traditional racquet, and have hitting surfaces ranging between 70 and 85 square inches in area.

The same principle used in choosing grip size and weight should be used in selecting racquet size. The players should choose the size that allows them to play at their best consistently.

Shoes

The selection of shoes is of great importance because of the sudden starts and stops and constant changing of direction required in tennis. Players should wear shoes that snugly fit the contour of the feet but do not pinch the toes, that have no pressure areas around the foot, and that provide support.

Balls

It is possible to purchase new tennis balls that do not have much life. To help protect players from this, many balls today are approved by the United States Tennis Association and will, in all probability, play well. When the can is first opened, a release of air should be heard; an absence of air release means that there is a chance that the balls do not have much life. If this is the case, they should be returned for an exchange. There are also pressureless balls, which usually come in boxes or bags.

When balls will not be used over a period of time, it would be wise to keep them in a pressure can to sustain their life a little longer. When the balls have become rubbery and bounce high, or when they have lost most of their bounce and are dead, they should be thrown away or used in some other activity.

SELECTION AND CARE OF RACQUETS AND BALLS FOR LARGE-GROUP INSTRUCTION

Tennis instructors at schools and recreation departments should encourage students to buy their own racquets. This will give them the opportunity to practice outside of class if they desire. Schools should provide racquets and balls for those who cannot afford them, however. This equipment should be returned after each period.

Racquet Selection and Care

Durable racquets should be purchased, since they will be used by different students during the tennis uints. The strung racquets priced under $15 are usually not as sturdy as those that cost more. Tennis teachers should shop around until they find a prestrung racquet that will hold up in their classes, especially when mishit, scraped on the court, and dropped. Wood racquets in the $20 to $30 price range can be suitable for group use. Be sure to ask for a school quantity bid, which should be 20 to 30 percent under single racquet price.

Consideration should be given to grip sizes and racquet weight of the racquets being purchased for large-group use. Most junior high school students have smaller hands than high school students, and would require racquets with smaller grips. In ordering racquets for junior high school students, the breakdown in grip sizes and weights that will accommodate most students is: one-third of the total in 4⅛ L, one-third in 4¼ L, and one-third in 4½ L. For high school classes, order 20 percent in size 4¼ L, 40 percent in size 4½ L, 20 percent in size 4½ M, and 20 percent in size 4⅝ M.

If possible, there should be five extra racquets per class. These will serve as backups in case of broken strings or frames. If necessary, physical education teachers can obtain some used racquets by sending a note to each student's parents, requesting that they check the attic, basement, or garage and donate racquets that have not been used in a long time. Surprisingly, many usable racquets turn up in this way. Be sure that the school principal, or administrative leader, has approved this procedure first.

To keep the tennis racquets in the best possible condition, players and teachers must take proper care of them. Some wooden racquets will have a tendency to warp if they become wet often and/or are kept in a damp area. Racquet presses can help prevent this possible damage. Metal racquets are protected by being covered when not being used and stored in such a way that stress is not placed on the handle or head. Composite racquets, though the most expensive, require less protection from heat and cold. Even so, they should still be covered and stored properly, as they are subject to chipping and string breakage.

Ball Selection

Pressureless balls are suited to school situations when they will be used over many months and then stored during certain parts of the year. The pressureless balls are usually heavier than pressure balls, but tend to keep their bounce for a longer period of time.

Many schools provide three tennis balls for each student, with the balls being returned after each class. However, students should be required to bring three additional balls for their use. This will allow every two students to have 12 balls with which they can practice the various strokes. Encouraging students to possess their own tennis balls will increase the chances of their practicing outside of class time.

Balls should be stored where neither excessive humidity nor dryness will affect their playability. While storage in cans is desirable for checkout and check-in purposes, a large cart (on wheels, if possible) is satisfactory.

OPTIONAL CLASS EQUIPMENT

If possible, portable tennis racks should be available. They can be purchased or perhaps made in the industrial science department. The portable racks will help store the racquets in an upright position and prevent any additional damage.

Ball storage baskets are helpful in keeping the tennis balls from scattering during storage. They also help make it easier to take the balls to and from the courts.

Ball-throwing machines, while expensive, allow students a lot of hitting practice, necessary in stroke development. Most of the machines vary in size, weight, ball capacity, and ball delivery rate. Some models have remote control built in, while others have it as optional equipment. Most of the machines available have speed as well as trajectory control. The majority of ball-throwing machines will need an electrical outlet, but it is possible to purchase cordless models.

Table 3.1
Tennis Equipment Sources

Bancroft Sporting Goods Co.	Prince Manufacturing Co.
Bancroft Court	P.O. Box 2031
Woonsocket, RI 02895	Princeton, NJ 08540
Donnay USA Corporation	Slazenger
P.O. Drawer 959	2522 State Road
Hanover, NH 03755	Cornwells Heights, PA 19020
Garcia Corporation	Wilson Sporting Goods Co.
Tennis Division	2233 West Street
329 Alfred Avenue	River Grove, IL 60171
Teaneck, NJ 07666	
	Yonex (distributor)
Penn Athletic Products	Marco Corporation
Chambers Avenue	1609 Grandby Street, N.E.
Jeanette, PA 15644	Roanoke, VA 24012

PURCHASING TENNIS EQUIPMENT

Although fluctuating equipment prices quickly make a printed price sheet obsolete, the information in Table 3.1 will enable you to contact some of the reputable companies, who will in turn send current catalogs. A letter written on your school stationery will bring a prompt response.

SUGGESTED CLASS/STUDENT PROJECTS

1. Obtain two current tennis equipment catalogs from different companies. Compare prices on 30 racquets suitable for class use, six dozen balls, portable tennis racks, and storage baskets (Ball Hoppers). Check for quantity discounts, and do not overlook freight costs.

2. Write to one tennis court construction company and obtain information (the surface they would recommend, how long it would take, the price) on a hypothetical four-court resurfacing project. (Be sure to indicate that this is a class project.)

3. Write to a tennis construction company and obtain information (surface, time to complete project, price) on the construction of four, six, or eight new tennis courts. (Be sure to indicate that this is a class project.)

4. Obtain estimates on the construction of a portable tennis rack that will hold 30 racquets.

5. Investigate the condition of the tennis courts at your school or recreation department or both. Check the court surfaces, net posts, nets, practice walls, and fences. What are your findings and suggestions?

4

Class Organization

Effective class organization can be the foundation for skill development in tennis classes, while the lack of such organization can make otherwise excellent teachers lose their effectiveness. Class organization is multifaceted in that there are concerns about safety, equipment, teaching techniques, and class formations.

SAFETY

The nature of tennis is such that there is always an outside chance that someone might be injured. Good class organization can help lessen that chance and at the same time reduce the likelihood of instructor negligence.

While it is impossible to eliminate all injuries in tennis classes, the following suggestions will help reduce the number of occurences.

1. Make sure that all players take a few minutes to perform some stretching and warm-up exercises.

2. Make sure that the students stand far enough apart so that they will not hit each other with the racquets during group drills.

3. Prohibit class members from attempting to jump the net.

4. Have students promptly pick up tennis balls lying on the court surface, especially where players are apt to be running.

5. Remove pieces of glass and other objects from the courts.

6. Point out the danger to others of throwing the racquets in anger or jest.

7. Suspend play or practice if the courts become wet and slippery.

8. Place the empty tennis cans wherever they do not pose a danger.

9. Require players to wear proper footwear.

10. Be sure that students look to see that their partners are ready before serving or stroking the ball.

11. Require players to take rest and water breaks during hot weather.

EQUIPMENT

This category is discussed more fully in Chapter 3. In summary, students should be encouraged to buy their own racquets and tennis balls because it enhances the chances of their practicing on their own. However, schools should provide racquets and balls for those who cannot afford them.

Each student should be responsible for taking a racquet and three of their own tennis balls to the class. The balls should be clearly marked as to their ownership. Students using equipment provided by the school have the responsibility of checking it out before class and checking it in after class.

INSTRUCTIONAL TECHNIQUES

During a tennis unit, the students are expected to develop physical skills that will improve their playing ability. They are also expected to increase their knowledge of the various aspects of the game. To be as effective as possible, the instructor must choose the instructional techniques that he/she thinks will help accomplish the set objectives. (See also the discussion of objectives in Chapter 2.)

Astute teachers realize that while some students may be visual learners and others may be auditory learners, most students use both of these methods to learn. Furthermore, students will not learn something fully until they experience it. Because of the different ways and combinations that people use to learn, instructors should offer alternative teaching-learning methods. These techniques should include lectures, demonstrations, exhibitions, drills, audiovisual experiences, and playing situations, in various combinations.

Lectures

While the lecture is probably one of the least effective teaching methods, some teachers attempt to relay most of their information in this manner. When speaking out of doors, the teacher must be aware of the elements and other possible distractions. In most situations, the instructor can arrange group formations so that neither the class nor teacher faces the sun or other possible visual distractions. Extraneous noise should be eliminated if possible.

Demonstrations

Demonstrations, if properly executed, can be an excellent means of teaching tennis strokes. Since incorrect demonstrations will give students the wrong impression, the demonstrator (teacher or qualified student) must conform to accepted techniques. Whenever there are left-handers in the class, the demonstrator must also demonstrate a correct left-handed swing, not necessarily hitting the ball. If a live demonstration cannot be performed in the proper form, the instructor must either "talk" the students through the correct swing or show a film.

Exhibitions

Occasionally, the situation may arise that excellent players, such as teaching professionals, can play an exhibition set or match for tennis classes at a school. It is also possible to ask members of the school's varsity team to play exhibition singles and doubles matches.

Advise the players putting on the exhibition as to the talent level of the classes. Ask the proficient players to use the strokes and strategies that would be appropriate at the various levels. Questions concerning the strokes and strategies can be answered when the players are changing sides of the net or between sets.

Drills

There are many drills used to improve stroke development. The advantage of a drill is that students can focus attention on one or two aspects of the stroke and thus gain skill. Various drills can be found in Chapters 5, 6, and 7.

Audiovisual Materials

The use of audiovisual materials is another way of helping students improve their skills and increase their knowledge of tennis. Most instructors have access to tennis books, magazines, films, videotapes, loop-films, magnetic boards, and chalk boards. These sources should not only be on standby for inclement weather but also be an integral part of the lesson plans and used whenever they would be beneficial to the students.

Playing Situations

After the basics of singles and doubles have been taught, students should be placed into game situations. It is then that the students and instructors can identify the individual student's strengths and weaknesses. Instruction, utilizing appropriate drills, audiovisual materials, and other instructional techniques, should be geared to the students' needs, as revealed by their play.

CLASS FORMATIONS

Many tennis instructors use group instruction when teaching the different strokes. To have good class control, the teachers will place their classes into rows, circles, semicircles, and scattered formations.

Outdoor Practice Formations

When teaching a large number of students, instructors must give thought to which formation will bring forth the best results. Regardless of the particular formation, however, students must be far enough apart not to hit each other.

Placing students in scatter or row formation usually makes it possible to observe the students easily. The instructor must stand far enough from the first row so that each class member in the formation can move into position to see him/her and vice versa. Left-handers should be placed on the right side (as the teacher looks at the formation).

Circular and U formations will cause some students to be behind or to the side of the instructor. The chances of observing and helping all students are lessened in these formations. They also make movement in unison by the group difficult to perform.

Small-group formations, such as one on two, one on three, and two on two, are often used by some instructors. Some of these formations can be seen in Chapters 5, 6, 7, and 10.

INDOOR PRACTICE STATIONS

Some tennis instructors have the option of conducting class indoors during inclement weather. At schools where tennis courts do not exist, the physical education teachers can teach the basics of tennis in the gymnasium.

Group formations, similar to those used outdoors, can be used to teach the different tennis strokes. When the students have learned the basics of the strokes, they can be placed at different stations to practice them.

Indoor Practice Stations for Beginners

Indoor practice, which is especially beneficial for beginners, should be arranged for serving, volleying, and ground stroking (see Fig. 4.1). The station method is recommended as it allows students to work on all strokes covered up to that point. It also allows students to spend more time at the stations where they need the most help. The class members are divided into equal numbered groups, if possible, and then they go to their assigned stations. Instructors should have preplanned how long

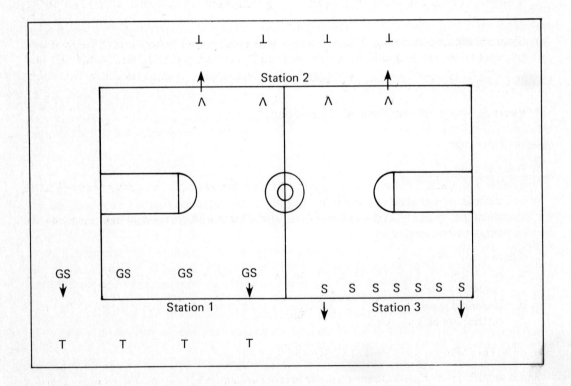

Figure 4.1
Indoor practice stations—ground stroke, volley, serve

a student is to stay at each station, and should advise the students when to change places in a situation as well as when to rotate stations.

Station 1 (Ground Strokes)

1. Tossers (T) stand with their backs approximately one meter (three feet) from the wall.

2. Ground stroking partners (GS) stand in the ready position facing the tossers, approximately nine meters (30 feet) away.

3. Students alternate throwing ten balls (underhand) in succession to each other (five forehands, five backhands).

4. Ground strokers are advised to stroke the ball back to the tossers with a full, smooth, easy swing.

5. Indoor sponge balls may be substituted where students lack ball control and can endanger class members.

Station 2 (Volleys)

1. Tossers stand with their backs approximately one meter (three feet) from the wall.

2. Volleyers (V) stand in the ready position, facing the tossers, approximately six meters (18 feet) away.

3. Students alternate throwing ten balls (underhand) in succession to each other (five forehands, five backhands). Balls should be at shoulder height for beginners and varied heights for intermediate and advanced players. Intermediate and advanced players should practice midline volleys (balls straight at their bodies) as well.

4. Fleece or sponge balls may be used at this station.

Station 3 (Serving)

1. Wall practice
   a. Limited space: Servers (S) stand approximately five meters (15 feet) away from and facing the wall; only fleece or sponge balls are used.
   b. Unlimited space: Servers stand approximately 13 meters (42 feet) away from and facing the wall; live balls are used.

2. Canvas backdrop practice
   a. Limited space: Servers stand approximately five meters (15 feet) away from and facing the curtain; live balls are used.
   b. Unlimited space: Servers stand approximately 13 meters (42 feet) away from and facing the curtain; live balls are used.

Indoor Practice Stations for Intermediate and Advanced Players

Intermediate and advanced players must continue to work at the ground stroke, volley, and serving stations, as these are basic to effective tennis. The three stations—half-volley, overhead, and lob— are to be used by experienced players (see Fig. 4.2).

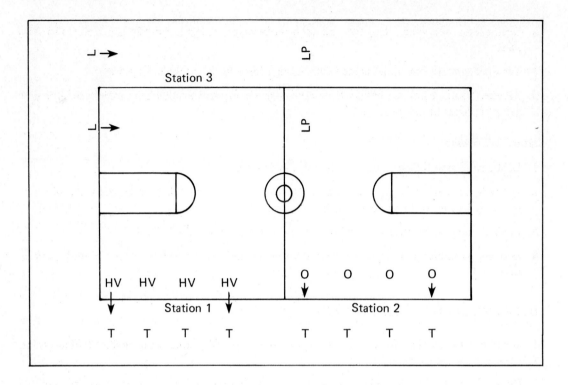

Figure 4.2
Indoor practice stations—half-volley, overhead, lob

Station 1 (Half-Volleys)

1. Tossers (T) stand with their backs approximately one meter (three feet) from the wall.

2. Half-volleyers (HV) face the tossers in a ready position approximately four meters (12 feet) away. A line one meter (three feet) in front of the half-volleyers is desirable.

3. Tossers aim the underhand throws at the line, to the forehand, and then to the backhand sides of the hitter.

4. Half-volleyers are advised to stroke the balls softly so that the tossers can catch them.

5. Students should use sponge rubber balls if live balls pose a danger.

Station 2 (Overheads)

1. Fleece or sponge balls only are to be used at this station.

2. Tossers stand with their backs approximately one meter (three feet) from the wall.

3. Overheaders (O) stand facing the tossers in ready position, approximately five meters (15 feet) away.

4. Tossers throw the ball underhanded with enough force to cause loblike trajectories.

5. Tossers should throw the ball so that the students can practice moving in different directions to get into proper hitting position.

Station 3 (Lobbing)

1. Lobbers (L) stand at one corner of the gym, hitting lengthwise.

2. Lobbers' partners (LP) stand approximately four meters (12 feet) behind the net and hit balls so that they bounce to the lobbers' forehand and backhand.

3. Lobbers can practice defensive and offensive (including top-spin) lobs.

4. Lobbers' partners should not return lobs with overheads, as that could create a hazardous situation.

SUGGESTED CLASS/STUDENT PROJECTS

1. Observe a tennis class for its safety aspects. Are any safety rules being violated? What can be done to help the situation?

2. Design a practice station alignment in a gym that has one basketball floor or two side-by-side basketball courts. Clearly indicate what would be done at each station, paying attention to safety aspects.

5

Beginning Tennis Instruction

Learning to play tennis is like learning to read. Although the concepts of reading are present in the first grade, the student may not be a proficient reader until the sixth grade. So it is in tennis. The concepts of stroking, game play, and strategies are presented in beginning tennis, and the student repeats and repeats until proficiency in tennis is acquired. Beginning tennis players do well to master the fundamental skills of grips, ready position, forehand and backhand ground strokes, forehand and backhand volleys, and the flat serve in 20 to 30 class hours.

These basic skills, covered in this chapter, will be described in terms for right-handed players, unless otherwise indicated. Teaching progression suggestions will be included for each skill. Progress will be speeded up if the instructor will give outside class assignments in the form of shadow drills and footwork drills that can be practiced in the student's home. Also, as the students work in pairs on the various drills in class, it must be stressed that the student putting the ball in play is working on his/her strokes just as much as the student receiving the ball; that is, if player A is working on the volley, and player B is ground stroking to player A, player B must make a full ground stroke using all the principles of good stroking.

GRIPS AND READY POSITION

Eastern Forehand Grip

Referred to as the "shake hands" grip, the Eastern forehand places the palm of the hand behind the racquet handle. This is the preferred grip for most tennis players, and recommended for beginners because the hand position is ideal for hitting balls at waist level and can be adapted for lower or higher balls. Unless otherwise indicated, the Eastern forehand grip is to be used on strokes made overhead or on the racquet side of the body. (See Fig. 5.1.)

Execution

1. Hold the racquet as near the end of the handle as possible so that the heel of the hand touches the butt of the handle. The racquet should be an extension of the arm.

2. Hold the racquet so that the edge of the racquet would touch the ground if the racquet were lowered.

Figure 5.1
Eastern forehand grip

3. Separate the thumb and index finger of the racquet hand to form a "V" on the top plane of the racquet handle, with the point of the "V" in the middle of the top plane.

4. Spread the first and second fingers to form a "trigger" finger, then grip the racquet firmly and "shake hands."

Eastern Backhand Grip

The Eastern backhand, like the Eastern forehand, is the preferred grip for beginners because of its added hand support on the back of the handle and its easy adaptability for hitting any ball bounce height. Unless otherwise indicated, the Eastern backhand grip is to be used on strokes made on the nonracquet side of the body. (See Fig. 5.2.)

Execution

1. Start with the Eastern forehand grip.

2. Support the racquet at the throat by the thumb and forefinger of the left hand, and rotate the racquet hand approximately one quater-turn to the left.

3. The point of the "V" formed by the thumb and index finger will be approximately on the line dividing the left and upper left planes of the handle.

4. Keep the thumb of the right hand around the racquet, or place it diagonally across the back of the racquet handle.

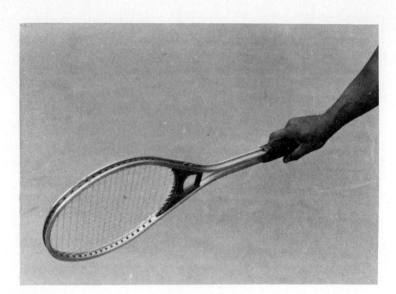

Figure 5.2
Eastern backhand grip

Continental Grip

The Continental grip offers one grip for both forehand and backhand. No grip change is required. Many players prefer this grip at the net where rapid volley exchanges may not allow the player sufficient time to change grips, and in serving because it adds spin to the ball. It is not recommended for overall play for beginners since it is best used to return low balls and does not adapt well to hitting all ball heights in ground stroking. (See Fig. 5.3.)

Execution

1. Modify the change from an Eastern forehand grip to an Eastern backhand grip by assuming a grip in between the two.

2. The point of the "V" formed by the thumb and the index finger will be approximately in the middle of the upper left plane.

Ready Position

The ready position is a side stride stance, facing the net. The receiver assumes the ready position when he/she receives a served ball, and during general play when he/she is uncertain on which side the ball will be hit. (See Fig. 5.4.)

Execution

1. Face the net.

2. Position the feet approximately shoulder width apart, with knees slightly bent and weight slightly forward.

Figure 5.3
Continental grip

Figure 5.4
Ready position

3. Hold the racquet in the Eastern forehand grip, supporting the throat of the racquet with the thumb and forefinger of the left hand.

4. Point the racquet head toward the net at or slightly above net height.

GROUND STROKES

Ground strokes are used to return serves and balls hit deep in the court after one bounce. (See Fig. 5.5, 5.11A, and 5.11B.)

Forehand

Execution

1. Use the Eastern forehand grip.

2. Take an early backswing.
   a. Begin the backswing as soon as the ball leaves the opponent's racquet.
   b. Draw the racquet back until the racquet head points to the backstop (Fig. 5.6).
   c. Have the left side to the net.
   d. Shift body weight more to the right foot.
   e. Lay the wrist of the racquet hand back so that the fingers of the hitting hand would point to the backstop if the hand were open instead of gripping the racquet.

3. Start the forward swing as the ball bounces.
   a. Step toward the net with the left foot, transferring the body weight to the left foot.
   b. Say "Bounce" as the tennis ball strikes the court, then the hitter will step-swing. Rhythm is BOUNCE-STEP-SWING.

Figure 5.5
Forehand ground stroke

Figure 5.6
Backswing, with fence as reference point

4. Contact the ball almost even with the left foot.
   a. Make sure the racquet face is parallel to the net.
   b. Try to see the ball contact the racquet strings.

5. Follow through high.
   a. Rotate the upper trunk until the racquet hand points in the direction the ball is to go.
   b. Maintain a firm grip so that the wrist and racquet head do not roll over.
   c. Raise the racquet arm until the upper arm and shoulder almost touch the hitter's chin.

Teaching Progression

1. **Self-hit (a ball put in play in a nonservice situation)**
   a. Students stand in scattered position, left side to the net, racquet in completed backswing position.
   b. Students imitate instructor in backswing, hit, follow-through without ball until the instructor judges that the majority of the students have correct performance. Errors in backswing and ways to correct them are detailed in Table 5.1.
   c. Students then practice a self ball-throw without hitting. The ball is thrown underhanded diagonally forward (toward the net) as far as the student would step toward the net to hit the ball and as far as the racquet and arm extends for the hit. Students having trouble

placing the ball in the proper stroking area should use the T formed by the singles sideline and baseline as a reference point (Fig. 5.7).

1) The student (left side to the net) stands in hitting position with the left foot touching the baseline and the racquet head in hitting position over the T.

2) The student reverse pivots (right foot) and faces the net.

3) The student throws the ball to the T point and is in position to step toward the net and hit the ball.

d. The instructor demonstrates the self-hit ball from the baseline, followed by the student's attempts. As the student completes the forehand swing, he/she must "freeze" and count to three to check body balance, and to note if the follow-through is correct. Point out that each student can see their follow-through at the end of the stroke. If the follow-through is correct and always the same, the student's chances for a consistent stroke are good. Consistent good strokes equal consistent game play.

e. Place students behind baseline for self-hit practice. No one is to return balls. Stress that the ball depth is to be beyond the opponent's service line. Students should count to three out loud as they "freeze."

2. **Receiving a ball on the forehand side**

a. Students in scattered formation face the instructor and assume ready position.

b. Students follow the instructor's verbal and visual cues in shadow drills without balls.

1) Step (or pivot) to the right (right foot) and backswing.

2) Step toward the net (left foot) and stroke.

c. Instructor/student demonstration.

1) Student stands in ready position on the baseline. The instructor stands at the net on the same side as the student, facing the student.

Figure 5.7
Ball drop, with T as reference point

2) The instructor throws the ball underhand, waist high, so that it bounces approximately two meters (six feet) in front of the hitter, to the hitter's right.

3) Thrower says "Backswing" as soon as the ball is released. Hitter says "Bounce" just as the ball strikes the court, and starts the forward swing.

4) The hitter must pose at the end of the stroke to the count of three and check the follow-through. On completion of the follow-through, the fist of the racquet hand of the hitter should be pointed in the direction the ball is to go (Fig. 5.8).

5) Place the students on court (groups of two, three, or four, depending on class size), two groups per court. Each group will have a thrower, a hitter, and if necessary, ball re-triever(s). Rotate positions after ten throws and continue until the instructor finishes observing each class member (Fig. 5.9).

3. **Moving to receive a ball on the forehand side**
   a. In scattered formation, students face instructor in ready position.
   b. Students mimic instructor in a four-step drill to the right, starting on the right foot. Note that feet and racquet move together (Fig. 5.10).
      1) Racquet starts back.
      2) Racquet goes back farther.
      3) Racquet is in backswing position, and body weight is on the right foot.
      4) From backswing position, step toward the net with the left foot, complete the forward swing, and slide back to starting position.
   c. Verbal cues would be "Run—two—three" (racquet back on "three"), "Step toward the net" ("four"), and "Stroke," "Slide back—two—three" (starting position).
   d. Repeat until performance is correct without a ball.
   e. Demonstration of throw and hit by instructor and student.
      1) Student stands in ready position just behind the baseline. Instructor stands at the net on the same side as the student.
      2) Instructor throws ball underhand, waist high, approximately two meters (six feet) forward of the hitter and four to five meters (12 to 15 feet) to the hitter's right.
      3) Thrower says "Backswing" as soon as the ball is released. Hitter says "Bounce" just as the ball strikes the court, steps toward the net with the left foot, and starts the forward swing.
      4) Stress that the run to the side stops when the ball bounces (most beginners overrun their balls). NOTE: The run may be any number of steps. The four-step drill was chosen for practice and out of consideration for the large class.
      5) Place students on court (groups of two, three, or four, depending on class size), two groups per court. Each group will have a thrower, a hitter, and if possible, ball retriev-er(s). Rotate positions after ten throws and continue until instructor finishes obser-vation of each student.

4. **Moving backward to receive a ball on the forehand side**
   a. In scattered formation, students face instructor in ready position.
   b. Students pivot or step right (on their right foot), then run toward the backstop to their right (no backpedaling), moving their racquets to backswing position during the movement.
   c. From backswing position they step toward the net with the left foot, complete the forward swing, and *run* back to starting position.

Figure 5.8A
Follow-through pose

Figure 5.8B
Backhand follow-through

Figure 5.8C
Two-handed backhand follow-through

Figure 5.9
Court position for toss-hit drill

   d.   Demonstration of throw and hit by instructor and student.
      1)   Student stands in ready position just behind the baseline. The instructor, facing the student, stands at the net on the same side as the student.
      2)   Ball is thrown overhand seven to ten meters (20 to 30 feet) in a high trajectory and lands on or near the baseline.
      3)   The student runs back as soon as the ball leaves the thrower's hands.
      4)   Student waits until ball drops to hip level, then makes a full stroke. Stress patience, and not reaching high for the ball.

Backhand

Execution (Fig. 5.11)

1. Use the Eastern backhand grip. NOTE: For a two-handed backhand, the left hand is placed next to the right hand on the grip. No grip change is required (Fig. 5.12).

2. Take an early backswing.
   a.   Begin the backswing as soon as the ball leaves the opponent's racquet.
   b.   Assume the Eastern backhand grip as the left hand starts to pull the racquet back.

Figure 5.10A
Ready position

Figure 5.10B
Run 1

Figure 5.10C
Run 2

Figure 5.10D
Run 3

Figure 5.10E
Step toward net and
ball contact position

Figure 5.10F
Follow-through

Figure 5.10
Four-step drill

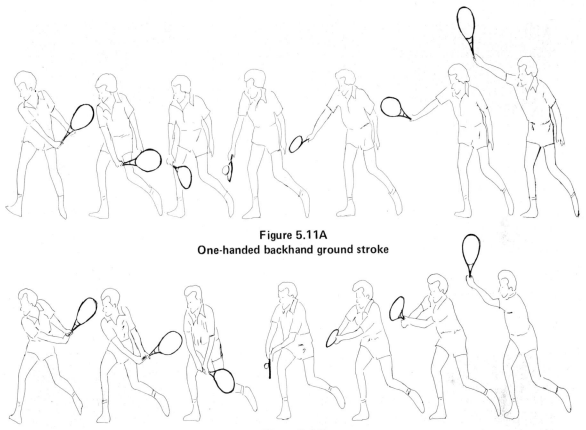

Figure 5.11A
One-handed backhand ground stroke

Figure 5.11B
Two-handed backhand ground stroke

Figure 5.12
Two-handed backhand grip

c. Continue to pull the racquet back until the racquet head points to the backstop.
d. Have the right side to the net.
e. Lower the right shoulder.
f. Shift the body weight more to the left foot.
g. Touch or almost touch the right hand to the left hip.

3. Start the forward swing as the ball bounces.
    a. Release the racquet throat with the left hand.
    b. Step toward the net with the right foot, transferring the body weight to the right foot. NOTE: For a two-handed backhand, the left hand maintains grip.
    c. Say "Bounce" as the tennis ball strikes the court, then step-swing. Rhythm is BOUNCE-step-SWING.

4. Contact the ball approximately one foot ahead of the right foot. NOTE: For two-handed backhand, the contact point is even with or slightly ahead of the right foot.
    a. Open the racquet face slightly. NOTE: For a two-handed backhand, the racquet face is parallel to the net.
    b. Try to see the ball contact the strings of the racquet.

5. Follow through high in the direction that the ball is to go.

Teaching Progression

Because the self-hit backhand is difficult for beginners, start with a thrown-ball drill immediately. Use Forehand Teaching Progression 2-3-4, pp. 25-29. Use Table 5.1 to help correct errors.

Additional Drills

1. **Two-hit and freeze drill.** Paired students face each other from opposite baselines. Each student has one ball. Player A stands in backswing position, ball in hand. Player B stands in ready position. Player A hits the ball to player B's forehand or backhand and "freezes" at the end of the follow-through so that the racquet hand is pointing at the nose of his/her partner. Player B decides whether the ball will be a forehand or backhand before the ball crosses the net and moves accordingly. Player B also freezes at the end of the follow-through, pointing the racquet hand at the nose of his/her partner. All players rotate one position to the left on instructor's signal. This drill enables students to "look" at their strokes. Stress early backswing and good follow-through.

2. **Continuous hitting.** After several rotations of two hits only, have the students try for four or more continuous hits. All balls are to bounce on or beyond the opponent's service line. Play is restarted when the ball bounce is out of bounds or in the service court area.

Strategies of the Ground Strokes

1. Be consistent—keep the ball in play.

2. Be deceptive by using the same general motion to hit the ball crosscourt, down the line, short, and deep.

3. Place the ball away from the opponent to keep the opponent on the run.

Table 5.1.
Ground Stroke Errors, Indicators, and Corrections

Errors	Indicators	Corrections
Late backswing	1. Late hit: racquet moves back as or after ball bounces 2. Ball flight to the right on a forehand, to the left on a backhand	Start backswing as soon as ball leaves opponent's racquet
Backswing too high	Underspin or slice balls	Place tennis can under arm that must stay in place during backswing
Too much backswing	1. Late hit (see above) 2. Racquet goes beyond fence reference	Use fence or wall to provide reference point for backswing (Fig. 5.13)
Side not to net (wrong foot forward)	Incomplete swing; "push" balls	Use reference points such as footprints and/or clock face numeral (Fig. 5.14)
Wrong grip on backhand	Ball flight high	Teacher checks grip change
"Wristy" swing due to loose grip	Uncontrolled ball flight	Use firm grip. Strengthen grip by squeezing sponge or discarded tennis balls 50 times a day
Rolling wrist at or prior to contact	Ball goes into net; racquet face is parallel to court	Freeze at end of follow-through and check to see that edge of racquet would touch the court
Ball contact too early	Ball flight to the left on a forehand	Patience! Say "Bounce" as ball strikes court, then step-swing
Does not hit through ball	1. Little follow-through 2. Ball flight might be high	Three-ball contact drill (Fig. 5.15)
Open face at contact	High ball flight	Check grip-stand at net and swing parallel to net with racquet parallel to net
Too much follow-through	Racquet goes too far to left	Use fence or wall to check follow-through (see Fig. 5.13)
Too far from ball	Reaching; may be late hit	Start movement to ball as soon as ball leaves opponent's racquet
Too close to (crowding) ball	Cramped swing and shortened stroke; no force	Check run to ball as ball bounces, then step-swing
Not enough follow-through	Short stroke; no force	Use reference points (pp. 27-28)

Figure 5.13A
Backswing, with fence as reference point

Figure 5.13B
Follow-through

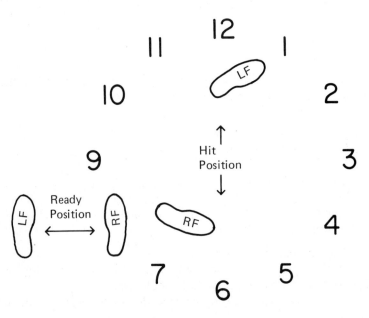

Figure 5.14
Clock reference point for positioning

Figure 5.15
Hitting through ball

FLAT SERVE

The serve is used to put the ball in play before each point in a game. The flat serve, using the Eastern forehand grip, is recommended for beginners (Fig. 5.16).

Execution

1. Assume a wide stride position, with the forward foot placed toward the intended flight of the ball.
    a. A line drawn from the toe of the back foot to the toe of the front foot would extend to the court in which the student wishes to serve (Fig. 5.17).
    b. "Draw the line" above by placing the racquet on court pointing to the service court toward which the student is aiming (Fig. 5.18).

2. Use the following four-count movements:
    a. Down on one—both arms start down and continue until the racquet reaches its lowest point next to the leg and the ball hand is in front of the thigh.
    b. Up on two—both hands start up on two with the ball being gently released at the peak of that hand's reach.
    c. Backscratch on three.

Figure 5.16
Flat serve

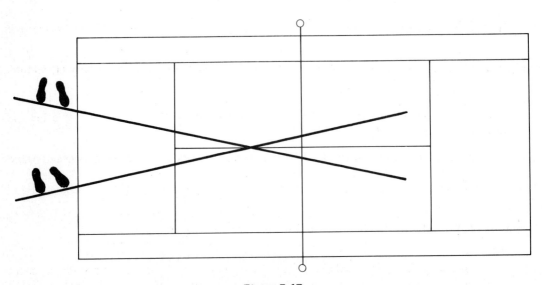

Figure 5.17
Straight-line reference point for server's foot position

Figure 5.18
Server's foot alignment, with
racquet as reference point

    d. Hit on four—start the overhand throwing motion as the racquet passes by the backscratch position.

3. Be sure that the ball is tossed as high as the fully extended arm, holding the racquet, reaches.

4. Contact the ball in front of the left foot.

5. Continue the follow-through in the direction of the court to which the serve is directed and down past the left leg.

6. On power hits, the right foot will step in the direction of the court to which the serve is directed.

Teaching Progression

  Since the ball toss is the most important part of the serve, begin instruction on it during the first tennis lesson. See Table 5.2 for errors in the serve and ways to correct them.

1. **Ball toss**
    a. Class stands (in correct service stance) facing instructor in scatter formation on court.
    b. Each student extends his/her racquet as high as possible with the racquet face parallel to the net and in line with the forward foot.

Table 5.2
Flat Serve Errors, Indicators, and Corrections

Errors	Indicators	Corrections
Ball toss over server's head	Ball flight over server's head	Eliminate "wristy" movement; release ball sooner
Ball toss too high	Pause at backscratch position while ball drops	Use extended arm racquet height as ball height measurement
Ball toss too low	Rushed swing; arm not extended at contact	Use extended arm racquet height as ball height measurement
Ball toss too far to right	Sidearm swing	Practice toss using vertical fence pole as guideline (Fig. 5.22)
No backscratch	Windmill swing or racquet head does not drop near shoulderblades	Bend elbow and loosen grip slightly
Early step with back foot	Eliminate trunk rotation; back foot contacts court before ball is contacted	Drag toe of back foot; no step at all with back foot for beginners
Follow-through stops too soon	Less power on stroke; racquet does not end up on opposite side of body	Continue motion until racquet goes beyond left leg; if necessary, hug the body
Head lowered before ball contact	Ball goes into net	Keep gaze up for a fraction of a second after ball is hit (Fig. 5.23)
Poor body alignment	Imaginary line extending from toe of back foot to toe of front foot does not point to proper service court	Use reference point (See Fig. 5.17)
Right elbow drops next to body prior to hit	Ball is pushed across court; little power	Use fully extended arm and racquet on ball contact

    c. The ball is pushed into the air as high as the racquet is extended and in front of the racquet so that it comes straight back to the outstretched throwing hand. The throwing hand should not have to move to catch the falling ball (Fig. 5.19).

    d. The student should attempt to put the ball in the correct place ten consecutive times.

    e. Assign home practice on this skill.

2. **Backscratch swing**

    a. Without a ball, class stands (in correct service stance) facing the instructor in scatter formation on court.

    b. Students place the racquet head between their shoulderblades in backscratch position (Fig. 5.20).

Figure 5.19
Service toss, with
racquet as reference point

Figure 5.20
Backscratch position

c. Students extend the racquet so that the racquet face is parallel to the net and in line with the forward foot (hit position).

d. Students rotate the upper trunk and swing the fully extended serving arm down to the left side of their bodies on the follow-through.

e. Repeat several times without tossing a ball.

f. From the scatter position, let those students closest to the net hit two serves. They then move to the back after their hits while the next group moves up to hit two serves.

3. **Full swing**

a. Class stands in scatter position in correct service stance.

b. With ball and racquet pointing to the court to which the student would be serving, the student swings down and up with both arms (counts 1 and 2) without releasing the ball (Fig. 5.21).

c. Student swings down, up, and backscratch (counts 1, 2, and 3).

d. Student swings down, up, releases ball, and backscratch (counts 1, 2, and 3). Student catches ball (count 4) instead of hitting it.

e. Repeat b–d as necessary until class is certain of the complete swing and ball toss.

f. Demonstrate the serve, using the four-count method.

g. Place the students in correct service position on courts and have them serve to the person diagonally opposite while the instructor gives individual help.

h. Stress the *full* tennis serve swing. If any student is unable to control the ball toss, however, start him/her in backscratch position until the ball toss is mastered.

Figure 5.21
Correct service stance

Figure 5.22
Fence post service toss guideline

Figure 5.23
Head up after service contact

4. **Court position for serving doubles and singles**
   a. Doubles—for overall play in doubles, the suggested service position is midway between the center mark and singles court sideline.
   b. Singles—service position in singles is as close to the center mark as possible on the correct serving side.

Strategies of the Flat Serve

1. Get first serves in whenever possible.

2. Hit serves deep into service court.

3. Hit serves to opponent's weakest strokes—probably the backhand.

VOLLEY

Volleys are used to return balls in general play, not on the serve, before they bounce. While advanced players may take a volley any place on court, beginners will have to be close to the net to learn the volley.

Some instructors prefer to have beginning students use the Eastern forehand and backhand grips and change grips when volleying. Others prefer the Continental, because the fast volley pace at the net does not always allow time to change grips. The ready position is the same as that for ground strokes except for the height of the racquet head, which should be just below eye level.

Beginners must be made aware that they will be volleying balls that will come to any of roughly four levels on either their forehand or backhand: shoulder, waist, knee, and ankle level. There will also be high overhead volleys and balls directed at the students.

Because the racquet moves in a punching rather than a swinging motion, there is little or no backswing and little follow-through. Therefore, the volley should be described in these terms: preparation, hit, follow-through, rather than backswing, hit, follow-through. See Table 5.3 for errors in the volley and ways to correct them.

Forehand and Backhand Volley

Execution

1. Stand in ready position, facing the net.

2. *Forehand:* Step in the direction of the oncoming ball with the left foot (Fig. 5.24). *Backhand:* Step in the direction of the oncoming ball with the right foot (Fig. 5.25).

3. *Forehand:* Lay the wrist back so that the racquet face is parallel to the net and in line with the oncoming ball. *Backhand:* Change to the Eastern backhand grip unless using the Continental grip so that the racquet is parallel to the net and in line with the oncoming ball.

4. Use little or no backswing and a short follow-through.

5. Contact the ball even with or slightly in front of the forward foot.

Table 5.3
Volley Errors, Indicators, and Corrections

Errors	Indicators	Corrections
Swinging at ball	1. Too much backswing	1. Student stands with back against fence
	2. Too much follow-through	2. Student stands facing fence, 1 meter (3 feet) from fence, and shadow volleys at a point on fence
Stepping with incorrect foot	Facing net	Practice foot patterns with shadow drill volleys
Ball contact not in front of forward foot	Late hit on ball	Student stands 3 feet from net and reaches across net to volley a tossed ball (Fig. 5.26)
Using wrong side of racquet on a backhand volley	Incorrect grip; palm of hand facing net on ball contact instead of back of hand	Student tries to use Continental grip so that no grip change is needed

Figure 5.24
Forehand volley

Figure 5.25A
One-handed backhand volley

Figure 5.25B
Two-handed backhand volley

Figure 5.26
Volley reach drill

6. Move the arm and racquet through a punching motion from the shoulder to approximately ready position.

7. Return to ready position.

Strategies of the Volley

1. Keep the volley deep unless you have a good angle shot.

2. Take a position at the net that bisects the opponent's angle of return (Fig. 5.27).

3. Move to meet the ball as high above the net as possible. Do not let the ball drop below net level.

4. Try a short volley if the opponent is behind the baseline.

SAMPLE DAILY PROGRESSION FOR BEGINNERS

Practice for 20 days of instruction is outlined in the following section. If a unit is longer than 20 days, continue to practice the basic skills presented in this chapter and include a singles tournament.

Day 1 starts directly with an activity. If tennis is scheduled as a fall sport, it may be necessary to precede the first activity day with introductions, announcements, discussion of class policies and objectives, and locker assignments.

Because class time is usually at a premium, warm-ups should be skill related. From Day 4 on, all warm-ups will be shadow drills with and without footwork over all the basic strokes. Shadow drills enable students to get the feel of racquet positions and court movement without a ball so that when the ball is used, skills are more easily learned.

Unless otherwise noted, students change places with their partners after ten throws or hits. In addition, they should rotate partners at least three times during a class period so that everyone learns to hit dirrerently paced balls and for good class interaction.

Finally, it goes without saying that all skills presented in class should be practiced on courts whenever possible, but the home assignments will eliminate the excuse: "I couldn't get to a court." These assignments are to be done 20 times each day, before the next class.

Day 1   Warm-ups
30-second eye-hand coordination test (p. 96)
Discuss racquet and ball selection and care (pp. 9-12)
Explain and practice forehand grip (p. 20), self-hit forehand (pp. 25-26), service ball toss (pp. 37-38)
Assign practice at home in service ball toss, shadow drill on self-hit forehand, concentrating on backswing, hit, follow-through positions

Day 2   Warm-ups
Explain and practice ready position (pp. 22-24), forehand hit of a ball thrown directly to the hitter, hitter starting in ready position (pp. 26-27), four-step drill (p. 27) with and without ball
Assign practice at home in shadow drill on forehand from ready position in place, shadow drill on forehand from ready position using four-step drill; continue to practice service ball toss.

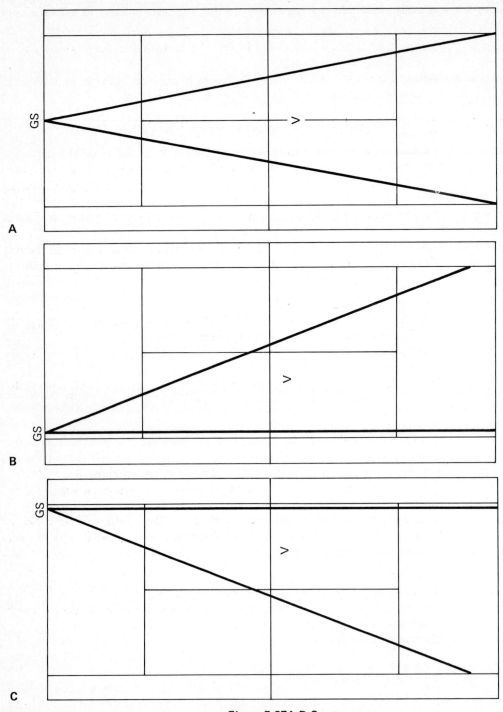

Figure 5.27A,B,C
Volleyer bisecting opponent's angle of return

Day 3

Warm-ups

Review forehand from the throw in ready position, with the four-step drill

Explain and practice backhand grip (p. 21), backhand hit from thrown ball in ready position (pp. 29-32)

Assign practice at home in shadow drill on backhand from ready position; continue to practice all assigned shadow drills except self-hit forehand

Day 4

Warm-ups

Review backhand from a thrown ball in ready position

Explain and practice backhand four-step drill without the ball, with the ball

Alternate ball toss to student's forehand and backhand, stressing early backswing and "freeze" on follow-through without running (pivot and step), with running (four-step drill)

Explain and practice flat serve, swing, and ball toss (without using balls) from back-scratch position (pp. 38-40), full swing (p. 40)

Assign practice at home in shadow drill on backhand four-step drill; and flat serve, full swing, and ball toss; continue practice on all earlier assigned shadow drills

Day 5

Warm-ups

Two-hit and freeze drill (p. 32)

Explain and practice flat serve (pp. 35-37); forehand and backhand volleys (pp. 42-45), using shadow drills and volleying from a thrown ball

Hand out simplified tennis rules, which are to be required reading before next class (Appendix I)

Assign practice at home in shadow drill on forehand and backhand volleys, flat serve, full swing; continue practice on all earlier assigned shadow drills

Days 6 and 7

Warm-ups

Alternate forehand and backhand hits from a thrown ball

Service practice

One demonstration doubles game, giving rules as play progresses (pp. 91, 118)

Doubles game play for everyone. This is primarily a rules-learning situation for the class

Assign practice at home: suggestions for the less skilled students should be made, using any of the shadow drills done. This assignment should be made for each student, as needed, from now on

Day 8

Warm-ups

Backward footwork movement without and with balls (pp. 27-29)

Two-hit and freeze drill, emphasizing an early backswing and freeze follow-through

Continuous forehand and backhand hitting

Serve and receive practice

Day 9

Warm-ups

Two-hit and freeze drill

Service practice

Serve and receive practice

Serve, receive, and keep the ball in continuous play as long as possible

Day 10	Warm-ups
	Practice skills test day (p. 94)
Day 11	Warm-ups
	Alternate forehand and backhand hits from thrown ball
	Serve and receive practice
	One demonstration singles game, giving rules as play progresses
	Game play, traditional scoring (p. 120). Those waiting should practice on the boards or score the game for those playing. Change opponents on instructor's signal
Day 12	Warm-ups
	Practice and game play as on Day 11, except score games using VASS (p. 121) in order to play more games
Day 13	Warm-ups
	Volley a thrown ball
	Volley a hit ball
	Doubles games, VASS scoring
Day 14	Warm-ups
	Stay on 21 singles (modified for class play to nine points) (p. 85)
Days 15 and 16	Warm-ups
	Skill evaluation (same tests as given on practice day)
Day 17	Written evaluation
Days 18, 19, and 20	Warm-ups
	Doubles tournament, VASS scoring
	Necessary written/skill test makeups

SUGGESTED CLASS/STUDENT PROJECTS

1. View a videotape of yourself performing the beginning strokes presented in this chapter. Record any errors and decide on correction techniques that would best apply.

2. Learn the basic rules of tennis and score several games played by classmates using traditional or VASS scoring or both.

3. Read two tennis articles that reinforce the instruction received on the ground strokes, volley, and serve.

Intermediate Tennis Instruction

New skills to be introduced at the intermediate level are the lob, the overhead (smash), the half-volley, and the slice serve. New strategies will include approaching the net when serving or receiving, playing side-by-side doubles, and poaching.

Beginning skills and strategies will have to be reviewed and will continue to be practiced. Consistency in using the skills taught earlier will be stressed even more at the intermediate level.

LOB

A defensive lob is usually hit from behind the baseline; it travels high and bounces deep in the court near the opponent's baseline. The apex (extreme height) should be over the opponent's service line for a good deep lob. An offensive lob is usually hit just inside the baseline, travels just out of reach of the net players, and bounces near the baseline. The apex of the offensive lob should be just behind the net player's head. (See Fig. 6.3.)

Execution (See Fig 6.1, 6.2)

1. Use the same swing as on the ground strokes except:
   a. Think "Slow motion" when stroking.
   b. Open the racquet face to a 45-degree angle.
   c. Follow through toward the desired apex of the lob.
   d. "Carry" the ball as long as possible on the racquet strings.

2. Hit the offensive lob with a more gentle touch and a shorter stroke than the defensive lob. (The ball flight should be lower). (See Fig. 6.3.)

Teaching Progression

The teaching progression for the lob is the same as for the forehand and backhand ground strokes (see pp. 25-29).

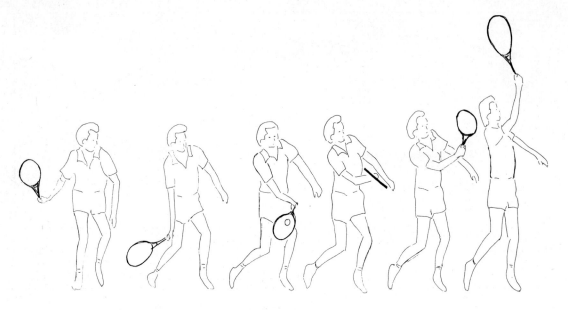

Figure 6.1
Forehand lob

Figure 6.2A
One-handed

Figure 6.2B
Two-handed

Figure 6.2
Contact points for backhand lob

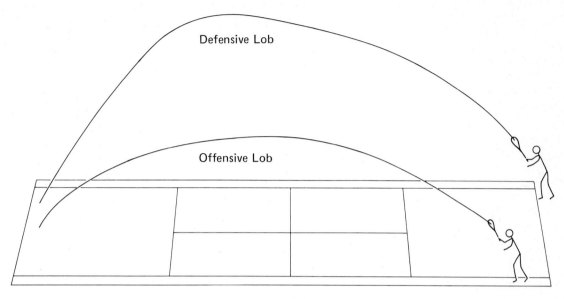

Figure 6.3
Lob trajectories

Additional Drills

1. Return a lob with a lob. Paired students face each other from opposite baselines. Player A hits a lob to player B, who returns it with a lob. Lobbing continues as long as the ball bounces in the back court. Play is restarted when the ball bounces out of bounds or in the service court area. Count the number of successful continuous lobs out loud.

2. Return a lob with a ground stroke. Paired students face each other from opposite baselines. Player A hits a lob to player B, who returns the ball with a ground stroke. Play continues in this way until the bounce is out of bounds or in the service court area. Count the number of continuous successful hits out loud.

   As the drills are performed, the instructor should observe the players, making sure that they position themselves to return the ball at approximately hip level.
   Table 6.1 details errors in performing the lob and ways to correct them.

Strategies of the Lob

1. Hit the lob crosscourt to allow more margin for error.

2. Use the lob:
   a.   When pulled out of position and needing time to get back.
   b.   When winded and needing time to recover.
   c.   To pass the net person.
   d.   To change the pace of the game and break the opponent's rhythm.

Table 6.1
Lob Errors, Indicators, and Corrections

Errors	Indicators	Corrections
Turning wrist over	Lower ball flight than desired	Open racquet face to a 45-degree angle; freeze at completion of follow-through
Ball flight too short	Ball does not go beyond opponent's service line	Increase force application; aim so that apex of lob is near or on opponent's service line (Fig. 6.3)
Ball flight too long	Ball lands outside court	Decrease force application; think "Slow motion"; "carry" the ball; see note on aim above

e. When the sun is in the opponent's eyes.

f. As an approach shot against a player who does not handle the lob well.

OVERHEAD OR SMASH

The overhead or smash is used to return lobs before or after the ball bounces on court (see Fig. 6.4).

Execution

1. Take an early backswing, sideways to the net.
   a. From ready position the racquet is lifted straight up with both hands as soon as the opponent contacts the ball.
   b. The racquet throat is released with the left hand, and the racquet head dropped to back-scratch position.

2. Point to the oncoming ball with the left hand and position the left hand and body in line with the path of the ball.

3. Start the arm-racquet extension as soon as the lobbed ball begins to descend, except on extremely high lobs.

4. Think "Service" and complete the stroke as you would a serve.

Teaching Progression

1. Students stand in scattered formation facing the teacher, who is on the opposite side of the net.

2. Students imitate the instructor's movements: backswing, hit, and follow-through without balls.

Figure 6.4A
Overhead, front view

Figure 6.4B
Overhead, side view

The instructor should observe to see that the students have eliminated the early wind-up of the serve. (Using both hands to lift the racquet straight up will prevent the "wind-up").

3. The instructor hits balls (one at a time) straight up in the air. The students go to backswing position and point to the ball with their left hands as the ball leaves the instructor's racquet. As the ball starts to drop, the students start arm-racquet extension and complete the swing. No ball contact is made. Students practice early backswing and full swing timing only.

4. Instructor/student demonstration. The instructor is on the baseline facing the student on the opposite service line.
   a. The instructor hits a high midcourt lob in *front* of the student.
   b. The student without a racquet takes an early backswing, points to the oncoming ball with his/her left hand, and moves until the ball can be caught high directly in front of the hitting shoulder with the right hand. Pretend that the right hand is a racquet and make a full swing.
   c. Repeat until the movement and body alignment are good, then have the student, with racquet, return the lob with a smash.

5. Instruct students to work in pairs. Each student is to catch five lobbed balls before any attempt to smash is made. Those students having trouble moving to the ball may practice catching lobbed balls on the ground outside the tennis courts. The overhead or smash is easier to learn if all lobs are placed in front of the one who is smashing.

6. Table 6.2 lists errors in the overhead and techniques for their correction.

Table 6.2
Overhead (Smash) Errors, Indicators, and Corrections

Errors	Indicators	Corrections
Facing net	Ball is "pushed"; loss of power	Think "Service" and assume same stance as when serving; check grip
Stopping follow-through too soon	Loss of power; ball goes into net or lands short	Pretend to throw racquet across net
Poor body alignment; ball would land behind player	Ball is mishit; ball flight is upward	Point at and/or catch oncoming ball, keeping it in alignment with and in front of hitting shoulder
No control	Sporadic good and bad hits	Use a medium swing; do not overhit
Lowering head before ball contact	Ball goes into net	Do not look at target area or opponent; keep looking up for a fraction of a second after ball is hit
Late backswing; too big a backswing	Mishit, rushed swing; ball flight is upward	Drop racquet to backscratch position immediately

Additional Drills

1. **Graduated length method (GLM).** For students having difficulty with overheads using the full length of the racquet. Paired students face each other. Player A stands in ready position mid-service court, while player B stands behind the baseline on the opposite side of the net. Player B lobs a ball to player A, who moves into proper alignment and returns the ball with an overhead while using (in progression) these actions:
   a. Gripping the racquet at the throat (Fig. 6.5).
   b. Gripping the racquet midway between the throat and the grip.
   c. Gripping the racquet at full length (at the grip).

2. **Alignment drill.** With racquet, take an early backswing, point to the oncoming ball with the left hand, and move until the ball can be caught without moving the left arm position.

Strategies of the Smash

1. In singles, place the ball away from the opponent.

2. In doubles, place the ball down the center of the court between the opponents.

Figure 6.5A	Figure 6.5B	Figure 6.5C
Throat	Midshaft	Full length

Figure 6.5
Overhead, graduated length method

3. Hit the smash before the bounce if possible to give the opponent less time to get into position for a return.

4. Hit the smash after the bounce when sun or wind is a factor.

5. Hit the smash after the bounce on an extremely high defensive lob.

HALF-VOLLEY

In a half-volley, the ball is hit on the rise just after a bounce. It is usually taken by a player approaching the net or who is in "no-man's-land," and the ball bounces near the player's feet.

The half-volley is a defensive stroke. If students are overusing it, check their court positions and footwork (see Figs. 6.6, 6.7).

Execution

1. **Forehand**
   a.   Refer to the face of a clock and, from ready position, backswing to 3 p.m.

Figure 6.6
Forehand half-volley

Figure 6.7
Backhand half-volley

    b.   Step toward the net with the left foot.

    c.   Contact the ball in front of the left foot.

    d.   Follow through to 12 noon or shorter.

2. **Backhand**
    a.   Refer to the face of a clock and, from ready position, backswing to 9 p.m.
    b.   Step toward the net with the right foot.
    c.   Contact the ball in front of the right foot.
    d.   Follow through to 12 noon or shorter.

Teaching Progression

1. Students who are in scattered formation, on the same side of the net as the instructor, imitate the instructor's half-volley swing without using balls. Think "Catch" at 3 or 9 p.m. and "Carry" to 12 midnight. Make a soft, controlled stroke.

2. Instructor/student demonstration. The instructor faces the student, each on opposite service lines.

   a. The instructor throws the ball to the forehand of the student, bouncing it just in front of the student's feet.

   b. Without a racquet, the student steps toward the ball and catches the ball on the rise, fingers up, with the racquet hand (Fig. 6.8).

   c. With the racquet, the student hits thrown balls to the instructor. The returned ball flight should be low across the net.

3. Pairs of students catch five thrown balls each before any attempt to half-volley is made.

4. On the backhand half-volley, the hand is not used to catch the ball. To practice moving without a racquet on the backhand, stop the ball on the rise with the back of the hand.

5. Table 6.3 details errors in the half-volley and their correction techniques.

Additional Drills

1. Player A stands in the middle of a service court in volley position. Player B stands directly opposite player A on the service line in half-volley position (Fig. 6.9). Player A puts the ball in play to the feet of player B. B returns with a half-volley, A volleys, B half-volleys, etc.

2. Players A and B stand opposite each other on the service line on one side of the court. The ball is kept in play by half-volleys. Play must be contained within the service court on the side of the court where the players are practicing.

Figure 6.8
Half-volley catch drill

Table 6.3
Half-Volley Errors, Indicators, and Corrections

Errors	Indicators	Corrections
Stance too straight; racquet head down	Ball goes into net; little knee bend seen	Bend knees until right knee touches court surface (Fig. 6.10)
Blocked ball; no follow-through	Ball goes into net	Racquet head should point to net at completion of follow-through
Body straightens as hit is made	Ball flight is too high	Keep weight forward and low
Racquet face is too open	Ball flight is too high	Practice proper racquet face angle; check grip
Trying to return ball as a ground stroke	Backpedaling as ball approaches	Stop all forward and/or backward movement as soon as ball leaves opponent's racquet

Figure 6.9
Volley, half-volley drill

Figure 6.10
Half-volley stance correction

Strategies of the Half-Volley

1. Keep the ball low.

2. Hit deep if the opponent is on the baseline.

3. Hit to the feet of a player approaching net.

SLICE SERVE

The slice serve is one that has mostly side spin, with a little top spin, imparted to it. It curves from the server's right to left (for right-handers) and is considered a fairly easy serve to learn. (See Fig. 6.11.)

Execution

1. Use a grip between the Continental and Eastern backhand.

2. Use same body alignment as for flat serve (pp. 35-37).

3. Place the toss the same as for a flat serve (pp. 37-38). Tossing it farther to the right would be an early giveaway to the receiver.

4. Bend the knees slightly, shift the weight to back leg, and coil the body slightly as the racquet is taken to the backscratch position with wrist cocked.

5. Forward swing starts by uncoiling the body as the racquet starts its upward movement. Body weight is being shifted toward front foot.

Figure 6.11
Slice serve

6. The racquet face meets the back of the ball, and the outward rotation in the forearm causes the racquet to move toward the right side of the ball (right-hander), causing a brushing effect.

7. The follow-through is helped along by the strong arm motion and the uncoiling of the body. This causes the server to take one step into the court with the back foot, and the racquet finishes on the opposite side of the body.

Teaching Progression

1. Experiment with the Continental and Eastern backhand grips and backswing into backscratch position. Select the one that enables the wrist to be cocked more readily. Practice the toss at the same time.

2. Holding the racquet with the Continental grip, the students should hit the ball so that it bounces hip height three times on the court. Hit the ball flat two times and, on the third hit, turn the forearm and wrist to the right to put side spin on the ball. The ball should be hit in front of the right foot. Continue until the students get the feel of the forearm-hand action. Students imitate the instructor in the mechanics of the complete slice serve without using a ball.

3. Use balls and practice hitting the slice serve. The arm and hand action involved in the slice serve can be compared to throwing a curve (slider) ball in baseball.

4. Table 6.4 details errors in the slice serve and their correction techniques.

Table 6.4
Slice Serve Errors, Indicators, and Corrections

Errors	Indicators	Corrections
Poor arm-wrist action	Little side spin; ball may stay to the right	Use a more vigorous outward rotation
Player does not open racquet face on contact	Too much spin; ball curves too much and has no power	Open racquet face on contact and continue forward motion as side spin is applied

Strategies of the Slice Serve

1. Use to crowd the receiver by serving to the receiver's left side.

2. Use to pull the receiver wide on the deuce court by serving to the right side of the receiver.

3. Use as a second serve for more consistency.

4. Use as a change of pace.

INTERMEDIATE DRILLS FOR MOVEMENT, STRATEGIES, AND CONSISTENCY

Movement drills should conform to this rule: the player moves while the ball is moving and hesitates when the ball is stopped (when the ball bounces or is hit by the opponent's racquet).

1. **Volley (ground stroke).** Player A stands in midservice court facing player B on the baseline. Player B hits ground strokes to player A, who returns the ball with a deep volley to the backcourt. Play is to be continuous as long as the volley lands in the backcourt on B's side (Fig. 6.12).

2. **Volley midcourt and at net.** Player A stands on the service line facing player B on the baseline. Player B holds two balls. Player B hits two consecutive balls to player A. A volleys ball number one from the service line, moves toward the net and volleys ball number two from the midservice court. No attempt is made to keep one ball in play so that A's forward movement is uninterrupted (Fig. 6.13).

3. **Three-ball net approach.** (Ground stroke, service-line volley or half-volley, and net volley.) Player A and B face each other from opposite baselines. Player B holds three balls and hits them one at a time as ground strokes to player A. Player B must hit the second and third balls as soon as A contacts the ball—no delay! Player A takes the first hit as a ground stroke, moves to the service line and takes the second hit as a midcourt volley or half-volley, then moves to the midservice square and returns the third ball as a volley. Player B makes no attempt to return A's shots, so that A's movement to the net can be completed without interruption (Fig. 6.14).

4. **Service hit and run.** Player A stands on the baseline midway between the center mark and singles sideline to serve. Player B is in receiving position. Player A serves the ball deep in player B's service court and runs straight toward the net, stopping when the ball bounces. Player B retrieves

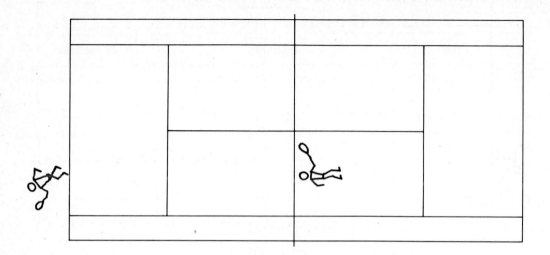

Figure 6.12
Volley ground stroke drill

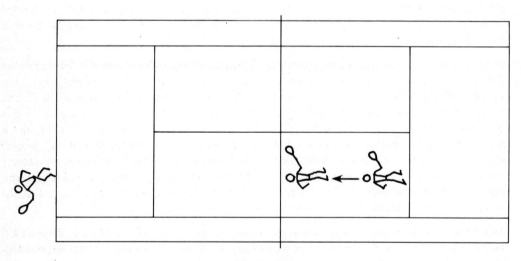

Figure 6.13
Two-ball drill volley midcourt, volley net

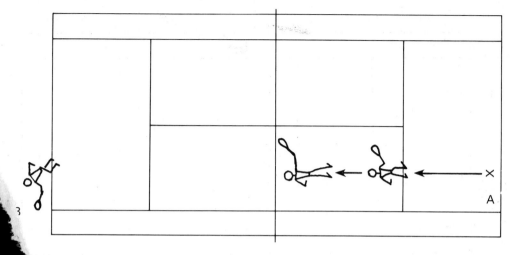

Figure 6.14
Three-ball net approach (back court ground stroke, midcourt volley, net volley)

the ball, and player A continues to practice "hit and run." Player A must not wait to see if the service is in or out, but runs immediately. The server should get to the service line by the time the ball bounces in the opponent's service court.

5. **Serve, receive, and come to the net.** Positions are the same as in Drill 4. Player B will return serve for continuous play in this drill. Player A serves, follows the ball to the service line, hesitates, returns the ball with a midcourt volley or half-volley, follows the ball to midservice court, and volleys. Player B also follows the ball as in the three-ball net approach practiced earlier, so that both server and receiver move to the net. All play is to be directed crosscourt with A and B hitting directly to one another. Player B should be holding two balls so that, if the serve or service return is not good, another ball can be put into play immediately and movement to the net will not be interrupted. Where players have difficulty with service return, instead of attempting a return of serve, the receiver should self-hit a ball as the served ball bounces so that the server volleys at the service line and movement is continuous (Fig. 6.15).

6. **Side-by-side doubles play.** Place four players on a court in suggested doubles position. Each player will serve four points in turn. The server and receiver must come in to the net immediately after they serve and return so that all points are played at the net. No lobbing in this practice.

7. **Ground stroke consistency.** Player A stands facing player B on opposite baselines. A rally is to be maintained on one-half of the court with the ball bounce in between the service line and the baseline. If the ball lands short or out of this area, play is stopped and started over. Count each rally out loud.
   a.   Repeat above crosscourt forehand position.
   b.   Repeat above crosscourt backhand position.

Figure 6.15A
Serve

Figure 6.15B
Move to midcourt

Figure 6.15C
Midcourt volley

Figure 6.15D
Move to net, volley position

Figure 6.15E
Volley

Figure 6.15
Serve and move to net

8. **Ground stroke "21."** For two players to practice singles, only the backcourt area is used, that is, that area bounded by the service line, baseline, and singles sidelines. The service courts and alleys are out. Play is started with a forehand ground stroke from anywhere on the baseline. Each player puts the ball in play five times in succession, so that every time the score is a multiple of 5 (5, 10, 15, 20) the service will change. Any error results in one point for the opponent. The first player to reach 21 wins. The entire game is ground stroking. Good hitting depth and backward movement are practiced in this game drill.

9. **Four-ball drill**. (Ground stroke, midcourt volley or half-volley, net volley, and smash). See Drill 3, p. 61. Player B holds four balls instead of three and hits the fourth ball as a lob.

SAMPLE DAILY PROGRESSION FOR INTERMEDIATES

Content for 20 days of instruction is outlined for the instructor. Longer units will give needed practice time to new skills and drills presented here plus a singles tournament.

Home practice assignments should be made on an individual need basis. As for beginners, warm-ups should be skill related and should include shadow drills and ball-hitting drills. Day 1 will start directly with an activity. It may be preempted if an organizational day is necessary.

Day 1	Warm-ups Subjective evaluation by instructor of students performing ground strokes and volleys Ground stroke evaluation: forehand and backhand shadow drills while the instructor observes and makes suggestions on backswing, contact point, follow-through, and footwork; alternate hitting ten forehand, ten backhand strokes from a thrown ball; two hit-and-freeze drills (p. 32), stressing early backswing, freeze follow-through; continuous hitting, first with the person directly opposite, then with the person diagonally across Evaluation of volleys, using shadow drills, then volleying from a hit (ground stroke) ball
Day 2	Warm-ups Concentrate on strokes from the day before needing most obvious help Review complete service swing and ball toss
Day 3	Warm-ups Serve evaluation by instructor as students practice Serving and receiving Serving, receiving, and continuous hitting
Day 4	Warm-ups Volley shadow drills, emphasizing balls hit at or below hip level Explain and practice midcourt (service line) volley (p. 61); two-ball drill volley (p. 61); three-ball drill: ground stroke, midcourt, volley (p. 61)
Day 5	Warm-ups Explain and practice half-volley: catch, then hit (p. 57); two-ball drill half-volley (p. 57); two-ball drill surprise half-volley or volley at service line

Continuous forehand and backhand ground stroking
Three-ball drill: see Day 4

Day 6   Warm-ups
Service practice
Explain and practice serving and coming in to the net behind the serve (p. 62);
   doubles positioning: play VASS games if time permits

Day 7   Warm-ups
Review and practice moving to the net behind the serve (p. 63) and moving to the
   net behind the service return
Play VASS games. Server and receiver must come in to the net behind their serves
   and service returns. No intentional lobbing

Day 8   Warm-ups
Explain and practice forehand and backhand backward movement for a ball thrown
   high. Emphasize stroking the ball at waist level or below and swinging from low
   to high. Do not reach for the ball (pp. 28-29)
Explain and practice lob (p. 49) and overhead (smash) before a bounce (p. 52)

Day 9   Warm-ups
Lob and smash review
Explain and practice four-ball drill: ground stroke, midcourt volley, net volley,
   smash (p. 65)
Doubles play, VASS, if time permits. Everyone must come to the net. No inten-
tional lobbing

Day 10   Warm-ups
Practice skills test

Day 11   Warm-ups
Review and practice forehand and backhand crosscourts, down-the-line practice
Explain and practice Stay on 21 singles, modified to 9-11 points for large classes
   (p. 85)

Day 12   Warm-ups
Singles play, VASS

Day 13   Warm-ups
Choice day: singles, doubles, or individual skill assistance

Day 14   Warm-ups
Practice at stations, individual help in serve; serving, service return, and coming in
   to the net; lob; smash
Game play (choice) if time permits

**Days 15
and 16**   Skills evaluation tests (same as practice skills test: see Day 10)

Day 17   Written evaluation of tennis terminology, rules, and strategy presented or assigned
   in class

Days 18,   Doubles or singles tournament, VASS
19, and 20   Necessary written/skills test make-ups

SUGGESTED CLASS/STUDENT PROJECTS

1. Observe a tennis game played by advanced players and rate the players' stroke performance on an analysis chart.

2. View a videotape of yourself performing three intermediate drills. Record any errors and decide on correction techniques that would best apply.

3. Interview a well-known tennis teacher in your community and write down his/her suggestions for tennis drills for beginners and intermediate players.

4. Observe and evaluate the teaching techniques of a teacher instructing a beginning or intermediate class.

7

Advanced Tennis Instruction

All previously learned skills will continue to be practiced. In addition, the scissor kick overhead and strokes using top spin, backspin, and side spin will be presented (Fig. 7.1).

TOP-SPIN SHOTS

A ball hit with top spin rotates away from the player who puts the ball into play, drops sharply into the opponent's court, leaves the court surface quickly, and travels a great distance. A properly hit top-spin ball has control and speed (see Fig. 7.2).

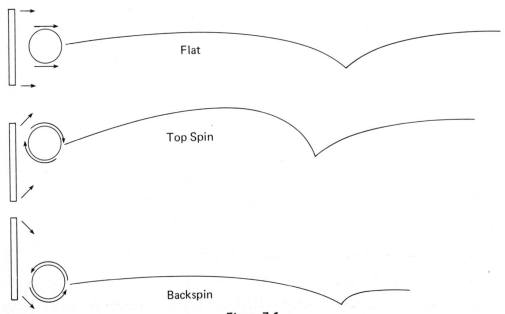

Figure 7.1
Ball reaction off racquet and surface of flat, top-spin, and backspin hits

Figure 7.2A
Forehand top-spin ground stroke

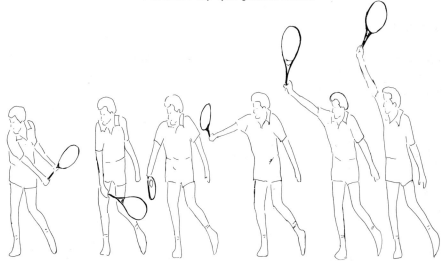

Figure 7.2B
Backhand top-spin ground stroke

Top-Spin Forehand and Backhand Ground Strokes

Execution

1. See forehand and backhand ground strokes (pp. 24-29)

2. Start the plane of the swing lower on the backswing and end higher on the follow-through.

3. Hit the ball with a flat racquet face, then brush the back of the ball with the racquet, passing up and slightly over the ball.

Teaching Progression

See forehand and backhand ground strokes (pp. 24-29). Table 7.1 lists top-spin ground stroke errors and correction techniques.

Additional Drills

Practice against a tennis backboard or with a ball machine is recommended.

Strategies of Top-Spin Forehand and Backhand Ground Strokes

1. If top spin is used against a net person, it will cause him/her to volley upward; the ball may then rebound high off the opponent's racquet.

2. Use these shots against an opponent who likes to slice or chop returns.

Top-Spin Lob

This is not a high-percentage shot, and only players with excellent top-spin forehand and backhand ground strokes should attempt it in competition (see Fig. 7.3).

Execution

1. See lob (p. 49).

2. Drop the racquet head below the level of the hand on the backswing.

3. Contact the ball even with the front foot, at waist level.

4. Use a fast whipping action of the arm and racquet.

5. Follow through high and directly overhead.

Teaching Progression

See teaching progression for the lob (p. 49). Table 7.2 lists errors in the top-spin lob and their corrections.

Table 7.1
Top-Spin Ground Stroke Errors, Indicators, and Corrections

Errors	Indicators	Corrections
Wrist turns over	Racquet face is parallel to court surface at end of follow-through	Exaggerate follow-through high immediately after ball contact so that racquet ends behind player's head on right side
Excessive top spin	Ball lands too close to net in opponent's court	Decrease speed on follow-through; hit more through the ball

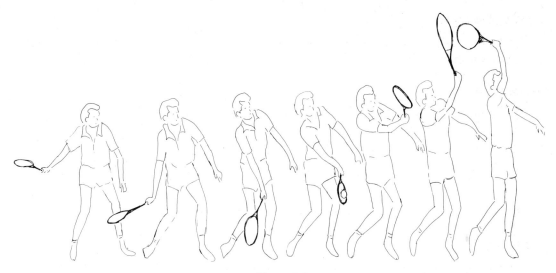

Figure 7.3
Forehand top-spin lob

Table 7.2
Top-Spin Lob Errors, Indicators, and Corrections

Errors	Indicators	Corrections
Ball too far toward net on contact	Reaching for the ball; little or no top spin	Improve body alignment so that ball contact is off forward foot
Ball too low on contact	Little or no top spin; difficult to initiate whipping action	Use top-spin lob on waist-high balls only
Excessive top spin	Ball flight shallow	Swing racquet upward and slightly forward through contact (see Fig. 7.3)

Additional Drills

Practice with a ball machine is recommended.

Strategies of the Top-Spin Lob

1. Use against a good net player early in the match.

2. Deceive the opponent by making the stroke look like a ground stroke until the last second.

3. Use on medium- or slow-paced balls that bounce to waist level to allow time for the whipping action of the forearm.

4. Use sparingly and for a change of pace.

Top Spin Serve

The top-spin serve, sometimes called the twist serve, is a high-percentage shot used by most good players—especially on their second serves. Top-spin serves are hit with a lot of top spin and little side spin. The top spin causes it to drop into the service court more easily than the flat serve. For right-handers, this serve will kick high and to the right. The student should have good control of flat and slice serves before starting to learn the top-spin serve (see Fig. 7.4).

Figure 7.4
Top-spin serve

Execution

1. Use the Eastern backhand grip. If this is not possible, get a grip between the Continental and the backhand position.

2. Use the same body alignment as for the flat serve.

3. Place the toss more to the left than for other serves. The ball should be over your left shoulder (right-handers) and not as high as for other serves.

4. Shift the weight toward the back leg, bend at the knees, rotate the trunk away from the ball, and arch the back as the racquet goes to the backscratch position. The wrist should be cocked as it gets to the backscratch position.

5. Rotate the trunk toward the ball as the racquet starts moving upward toward the ball. The body weight starts moving to the front leg.

6. Contact the ball at the lower left side and go up and over the upper right part with a brushing effect. There should be a strong forearm movement (outward rotation of the forearm) on this serve.

7. The first part of the follow-through will be higher and wider than with the other serves. The rest of the follow-through will cause a natural move forward with a step onto the court. The racquet should finish on the opposite side of the body.

Teaching Progression

1. Students, in scattered formation, face the instructor and practice the first part of the swing while using the Continental grip. The ball is tossed so that it drops toward the left shoulder. At the same time, the knees are bent, the trunk is rotated, and the back is arched. Get the racquet to the backscratch position with the wrist cocked. The ball is not hit.

2. Holding the racquet with the backhand or Continental grip, the students should hit the ball from hip height onto the court three times. The ball is to be hit flat two times; on the third hit, the racquet is rolled over the ball so that top spin is applied. The ball should be hit in front of the left foot.

3. Go through the complete top-spin swing without using balls.

4. Use balls and practice serving balls with top spin.

    Table 7.3 lists errors in the top-spin serve and their corrections.

Strategies of the Top-Spin Serve

1. Use as a dependable second serve.

2. Use as a change-of-pace first serve.

3. Use to crowd the receiver by serving to the receiver's right side.

4. Use to pull the receiver wide on the ad court by serving to the left side of the receiver.

Table 7.3
Top-Spin Serve Errors, Indicators, and Corrections

Errors	Indicators	Corrections
Racquet not going up and over ball	Ball does not bounce high, lacks top spin	Give server reference points on ball: e.g., pretend ball is a clock and contact it at 7 o'clock, then hit up and over to 1 o'clock
Going over ball too soon	Ball drops too fast and usually short	Servers must wait until they make contact at 7 o'clock before starting vigorous forearm-wrist action

BACKSPIN (UNDERSPIN) SHOTS

A ball hit with backspin rotates toward the player who puts the ball into play, appears to "float" above the court surface, and bounces short and low. When hit with excessive backspin, the ball may even bounce backward, away from the opponent. The drop shot, chop, and drop volley are all hit with backspin. These are low-percentage, occasional strokes, used for a change of pace. An advanced player can win without using them.

Drop Shot

Execution

1. See forehand and backhand ground strokes (pp. 24-29).

2. Open the racquet face on ball contact.

3. Brush under the ball, using a down and forward motion.

4. Decrease the speed of the racquet and shorten the follow-through.

5. Disguise the stroke until the last second by using the same backswing as for a forehand or backhand ground stroke.

6. Give with the racquet and arm against a fast ball to absorb some of the force.

Teaching Progression

1. Students, in scattered formation facing the instructor on the same side of the court, imitate the instructor's movements—backswing, hit, follow-through—without hitting any balls.

2. Instructor/student demonstration. The instructor is at midservice court facing the student on the opposite service line.

Table 7.4
Drop Shot Errors, Indicators, and Corrections

Errors	Indicators	Corrections
Racquet face too open	Ball crosses net high	Practice correct racquet angle without using a ball
Punching the ball	Ball goes too deep in court	Brush back of ball, using a less firm grip

a. The instructor throws a medium-paced ball to the student's forehand.
b. The student steps toward the ball, opens the racquet face, and catches the ball on the racquet strings after the first bounce.
c. The student uses an abbreviated swing and an open racquet face on the next ball thrown.
d. The student increases the length of the swing and adjusts the open racquet face until a desirable ball flight is obtained.

4. Instruct students to work in pairs. Each student is to follow the progression demonstrated for the forehand and backhand drop. Table 7.4 details the errors in the drop shot and their corrections.

Strategies of the Drop Shot

1. Use against a weak second serve.

2. Use against a slow back-court player.

3. Use sparingly for a change of pace.

4. Use early in the match.

5. Use when the hitter can afford to lose a point.

Chop

Execution

1. Take the racquet back higher than the ball level on the backswing.

2. Swing forward and down, meeting the ball even with, or just in front of, the forward foot.

3. Hit just underneath the back part of the ball and continue the forward-down motion.

Teaching Progression

1. Students, in scattered formation on court, face the instructor and imitate the swing without the use of balls.

2. Students pretend to chop down a tree, using a forward-downward movement of the racquet.

Table 7.5
Chop Errors, Indicators, and Corrections

Errors	Indicators	Corrections
Swing is straight down	Much underspin but a weak shot	Swing forward as well downward
Poor racquet face positioning: closed	Ball goes into net	Practice stroke without a ball, paying close attention to racquet face position
Poor racquet face positioning: open	Ball goes too high	Practice stroke without a ball, paying close attention to racquet face position

3. Instructor/student demonstration:
   a. The instructor stands in ready position, midservice court. The student stands facing the instructor on the opposite side of the net, midservice court.
   b. The student throws the ball underhand slow and easy so that it bounces low and to the hitter's right or left.
   c. The instructor demonstrates forehand and backhand chop shots from this position.
   d. The instructor moves to the service line and repeats hits.
   e. The instructor moves to the baseline and repeats hits.

4. Paired students follow the same sequence.

5. Students practice returning soft serves with a chop. Table 7.5 lists errors in the chop and details techniques for their correction.

Strategies of the Chop

1. Use to return a hard fast serve.

2. Use against players who do not return low balls well.

3. Use in a rally to change the pace of balls hit hard by opponents.

Drop Volley

Execution

1. See the volley (p. 42).

2. Open the racquet face slightly.

3. Use an abbreviated high-to-low swing with a sharp follow-through.

4. Loosen the grip slightly against a hard-hit ball.

Table 7.6
Drop Volley Errors, Indicators, and Corrections

Errors	Indicators	Corrections
Too much backswing and follow-through	Volley goes too deep	Use fence correction described under regular volley (p. 43)
Racquet face too open	Volley goes too high	Check grip; practice getting racquet into proper angle without using a ball

Teaching Progression

1. Instructor demonstrates and the students imitate the movements of the drop volley.

2. Instructor/student demonstration. The instructor is in the midservice court facing the student on the opposite service line.
   a. The student throws the balls underhand approximately waist high and to the right or the left of the instructor.
   b. The instructor hits forehand and backhand drop volleys.

3. Paired students practice forehand and backhand drop volleys from thrown balls.

4. Paired students practice drop volleys from hit balls. One student stands on the baseline and hits ground strokes to the partner at the net, who returns the ball with a drop volley whenever possible. Table 7.6 lists errors in the drop volley and their corrections.

Strategies of the Drop Volley

1. Use against a slow-moving player.

2. Use against an opponent who stays well behind the baseline.

SIDE-SPIN SHOTS

Side-spin shots are those that spin from left to right or from right to left (on a horizontal plane). The slice serve (p. 59) is the most widely used side-spin stroke, but some players will use side spin on ground strokes and volleys as well (see Fig. 7.5).

Ground Stroke with Side Spin (Slice)

Execution

1. To curve the ball from left to right, the racquet action will be from right to left (forehand). Imagine that the ball is a clock and brush the back of the ball with the racquet strings by moving the racquet from 3 o'clock to 9 o'clock.

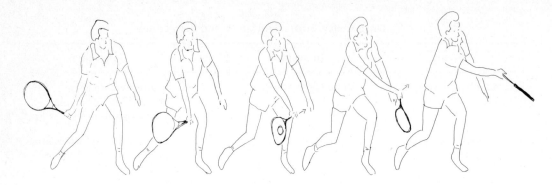

Figure 7.5
Side-spin ground stroke

Table 7.7
Ground Stroke with Side-Spin (Slice) Errors, Indicators, and Corrections

Errors	Indicators	Corrections
Not using side-spin stroke	Ball spins very little and does not curve	Use more horizontal action during swing
Too much brushing	Ball curves too much and goes out of bounds	Swing through ball as well as sideways

2. To curve the ball from right to left, the racquet action will be from left to right (backhand). The racquet face should brush the ball from 9 o'clock to 3 o'clock.

Teaching Progression

1. Students stand in scattered formation facing the instructor on the same side of the court.

2. Students imitate the instructor's forehand and backhand strokes with the racquet moving in a horizontal plane.

3. Instructor/student demonstration. The student stands at the net, his/her back to the net, facing the instructor standing on the baseline. The student throws a medium-paced ball to the instructor's forehand and backhand.

4. Paired students imitate the instructor/student demonstration. Table 7.7 lists errors in the ground stroke with side spin (slice) and their corrections.

Strategies of the Ground Stroke With Side Spin (Slice)

1. Hit side-spin shots so that they curve into and crowd the opponent.

2. Hit side-spin shots to pull the opponent wide and into poor court position.

Figure 7.6
Scissor kick overhead

SCISSOR KICK OVERHEAD SHOT (SMASH)

The scissor kick overhead or smash is a shot used when an offensive lob has been hit and the player in the volley position cannot hit it without jumping up from the court. It is at this point that the player leaps in a backward direction, with a scissor kick effect, and executes the overhead (see Fig. 7.6).

Execution

1. From the ready volley position, the player straightens up when he/she notices the offensive lob trajectory.

2. The first step (right-handers) is with the right foot, which steps backward, and the racquet starts moving up on the way to backscratch position.

3. The right knee bends slightly and straightens to spring the body upward and backward.

4. While the body is in the air, the racquet arrives at backscratch position, and the right foot moves forward as the left foot moves back in a scissors effect.

5. The racquet moves up and forward to make contact with the ball. The wrist snaps upon contact, and then the left foot makes contact with the court.

6. The right foot contacts the court as the follow-through ends with the racquet finishing on the opposite side of the body.

Teaching Progression

1. Students, in scattered formation, stand in volley position and take a step back with the right foot as they spring up and back. The racquet goes into backscratch position. This move is repeated until it can be performed with ease.

2. Step 1 is repeated with the scissor kick-swing portion of the overhead added. This is repeated without using any balls.

3. Once the motion of the scissor kick overhead is learned, practice it using balls for timing and control.

Table 7.8 lists errors in the scissor kick overhead shot (smash) and their corrections.

Strategies of the Scissor Kick Overhead

See the smash (p. 54).

ADVANCED DRILLS FOR MOVEMENT, STRATEGIES, AND CONSISTENCY

In addition to the drills given below, the drills given for the intermediate level and in Chapter 10 should be used at the advanced level as well.

Table 7.8
Scissor Kick Overhead (Smash) Errors, Indicators, and Corrections

Errors	Indicators	Corrections
Hitting ball too late	Ball hit behind head; it goes long	Prepare sooner; meet ball earlier
Poor timing on takeoff	Hitting ball on racquet tip; player landing before ball is hit	Watch ball closely

Two-on-One-Drills

1. **Net player versus two baseline players.** The baseline players hit ground strokes to the net player who returns the balls with deep volleys. Play should be continuous, with the baseliners attempting to pass or lob the net person occasionally. VARIATION: Net player accuracy. The baseline players hit directly to the net player, who alternates hitting back to the court corners. (Fig. 7.7).

2. **Baseline player versus two net players.** The net players hit deep volleys to the baseliner's back-court, keeping the baseliner moving from side to side. Play should be continuous so that the baseliner has to scramble to make good returns (Fig. 7.8).

3. **Poaching.** Two baseliners stand in serve-receive position on courts. One net player stands on the server's side, midservice court. The player in service position ground strokes the ball to the receiver who returns the ball crosscourt only. The net player intercepts all balls possible. The baseliners work on their crosscourt consistency. No down-the-line shots are allowed. The net player is to move for every ball. CUE: as the baseline player facing the net player contacts the ball, the net player starts to move center court. The net player should say "Hit" just as the base-liner contacts the ball, then step and reach for the ball. If the baseliners are successful in passing the net player, the net player moves back to midservice court immediately. Ground stroking is to be continuous (Fig. 7.9).

    VARIATION 1: Put the ball in play with a serve and continue as in the previous drill.

    VARIATION 2: Put the ball in play with a ground stroke or a serve and allow down-the-line or passing shots.

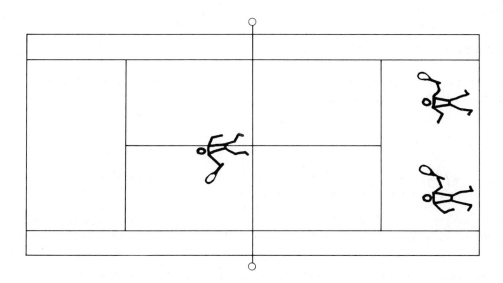

Figure 7.7
One net player versus two baseline players

Figure 7.8
One baseline player versus two net players

Figure 7.9
Poaching

Return of Serve

1. **Short service.** The server stands on the service line, midservice court. The receiver stands in receiving position on the baseline. The server serves a ball with pace to the receiver, who must react quickly to make a good crosscourt return. The receiver always tries to take a full backswing. If the serve is too hard and fast, however, the receiver will return the ball with a stroke similar to the half-volley—"catch (i.e., grip hard) and carry" (see p. 57). The stroke will not have as much force as one that is hit by a player taking a full backswing. Players should remember that, in doubles, the receiver wants to return the ball to the server's feet as the server approaches the net; in order to do so, the backswing may be abbreviated (Fig. 7.10).

2. **Crowding the server.** The server stands on the baseline in doubles service position. The receiver stands two to three feet inside the baseline. The server serves good second serves, then the receiver returns all balls crosscourt (Fig. 7.11).

   Both of the drills above should improve the receiver's reaction time and make the receiver more alert to the server's movements. Stress watching the ball, not the server.
   VARIATION: Work on serve and receive from doubles position, keeping all balls crosscourt.

Net, One-on-One

Down the line, crosscourt at the net. Players position themselves inside a service court facing each other. Balls and players must stay within the service courts. Players keep the balls in play using drop shots, drop volleys, and half-volleys as they attempt to go down the line and crosscourt.

Figure 7.10
Short serve drill

Figure 7.11
Crowding server

Smash-Lob

The net player faces a baseline player. The baseline player alternates hitting short lobs and long lobs so that the net player is forced to move back and up.

Net Approach and Overall Court Coverage

Six-ball drill. Players stand facing each other on opposite baselines. Player B holds six balls and hits them consecutively to player A, who takes the first ball as a ground stroke, moves to midcourt and takes the second ball with a volley or half-volley, and moves to net position and returns the third ball as a volley. Player B lobs the fourth ball just behind player A so that A must move back for a smash, then A recovers to take two volleys.

SAMPLE DAILY PROGRESSION FOR ADVANCED STUDENTS

Suggestions for 20 days of instruction for the advanced player are outlined on the following pages. Skill-related warm-ups for this group may be selected from those presented in Chapter 6 (on intermediate instruction) or Chapter 10 (on coaching).

Day 1   Warm-ups
Review and practice continuous forehand and backhand ground stroke rally, minimum goal; 12 consecutive hits; net volleys, midcourt volley, and half-volleys; three-ball drill: ground stroke, midcourt volley, and volley (p. 61)

Day 2   Warm-ups
Review and practice continuous volley at the net, continuous volley from the service line, lob, smash
Explain and practice six-ball drill: ground stroke, midcourt volley, net volley, half-court smash, midcourt volley, net volley (p. 84)

Day 3   Warm-ups
Explain and practice poaching (p. 81), two-step-in drill (p. 115)
Review and practice flat serve, side-spin serve

Day 4   Warm-ups
Discuss good doubles play and positioning
Choice of doubles play or individual skill assistance

Day 5   Warm-ups
Explain and practice top-spin serve (p. 73), receiving (p. 83), two-on-one baseline ground stroking (p. 81)

Day 6   Warm-ups
Practice serving, receiving, and continuous hitting; serving, receiving, and both coming in to the net
Doubles games, VASS scoring

Day 7   Warm-ups
Choice day: singles, doubles, or individual skill assistance

Day 8   Warm-ups
Practice forehand and backhand ground stroke (continuous rally)
Stay on 21 singles (p. 65)

Day 9   Warm-ups
Practice serving and receiving
Explain and practice serving and moving in to the net in singles game play
Discuss singles strategy
Singles game play, VASS scoring

Day 10   Warm-ups
Choice day: singles, doubles, or individual skill assistance

Day 11   Warm-ups
Practice skills test and/or practice at stations

Day 12   Warm-ups
Practice two-step-in drill; serving, receiving, and coming in to the net
Play singles or doubles

Day 13	Warm-ups
	Practice two-step-in drill; serving, receiving, and coming in to the net
	Explain and practice two-on-one volley drill, Australian doubles (p. 92)

Days 14 and 15	Warm-ups
	Skill evaluation tests (same as practice test)

Day 16	Written evaluation

Days 17, 18, and 19	Warm-ups
	Doubles or singles tournament, VASS scoring
	Necessary written/skills test make-ups

Day 20	Challenge day

SUGGESTED CLASS/STUDENT PROJECTS

1. Design three drills for practicing any of the skills of tennis and teach one of them to class members for evaluation.

2. Make a videotape of two beginning tennis players and analyze their strengths and weaknesses. Suggest correction techniques and practice drills that would improve the players' performance.

3. Observe and evaluate the teaching techniques of a teacher instructing an intermediate and/or advanced class.

4. Observe an exhibition set played by expert players. After the set, have a group discussion about observed stroking techniques. Class members can then direct the players to hit certain shots for further observation. Discuss which segments of the demonstration were most beneficial to the class and why.

Tennis Strategy

SINGLES STRATEGY

Starting Positions

The server stands behind the baseline one meter or less (one to three feet) to the right or left of the center mark, depending on whether the serve is to the deuce or the ad court.

The receiver stands approximately one meter (three feet) behind the baseline in the position that allows him/her to have half the service court to the right and half to the left side (Fig. 8.1).

Beginning Singles

The strategies of play in singles used by beginners relate to whether they are serving, returning serve, or playing from the backcourt. Player strategy in each of these situations is described below.

1. When serving:
   a. Get the first serve in as often as possible. For some players, this means not hitting the serve as hard.
   b. Try to hit the serve deep into the opponent's service court.
   c. Direct the serve at the opponent's weak stroke (usually the backhand).

2. When receiving:
   a. Move and hit with the strongest stroke when the serve is coming toward the midline.
   b. Return most serves deep and, if possible, crosscourt.
   c. Stand in front of the baseline to return weak serves and then move to the ready position behind the center mark.

3. When in the backcourt:
   a. Concentrate on keeping the ball in play.
   b. Attempt to hit most of the shots past the opponent's service line.
   c. Hit as many shots as possible to the opponent's weakness (probably the backhand).
   d. Avoid staying in "no-man's-land" (the area between the volley position and the baseline) (Fig. 8.2). Being caught in this area will usually result in balls hit near the feet, thus making them difficult to return.)

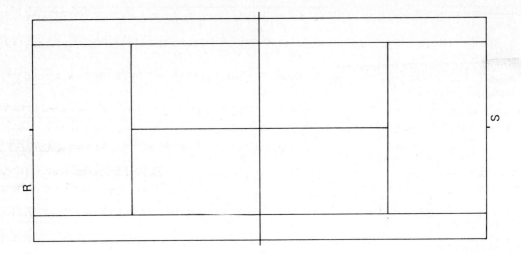

Figure 8.1
Singles starting positions

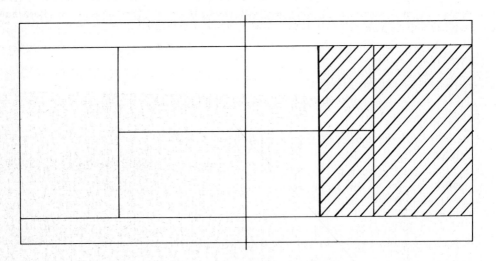

Figure 8.2
No-man's-land, area between the volley position and the baseline

Intermediate and Advanced Singles

The play systems used by intermediate and advanced players include serve and volley, return of serve, and backcourt and all-court play. This type of play is more aggressive and played at a faster pace than beginners singles play.

1. Serve and volley
   a. Continue to get the first serve in, using spin on the ball if possible.
   b. Vary the type of serves hit, but direct most of them to the opponent's weak stroke.
   c. Attempt to hit the serves deep into the opponent's service court.
   d. Plan ahead when moving to the net behind the serve.
   e. Make the first volley (from the service line) a deep one and then move into the regular volley position.
   f. Angle the second volley, trying to get the opponent out of position.
   g. Move in behind the second serve only if it has been effective.

2. Return of serve
   a. Continue to concentrate on keeping the ball in play.
   b. Return crosscourt and deep unless the server is moving to volley position after the serve.
   c. Attempt to return the serve low if the server moves in after the serve.
   d. Exploit an opponent's weakness with the return of serve; continue to "hammer away" as long as it pays off.
   e. Vary the returns (top-spin, backspin, crosscourt, and down-the-line shots) if the server moves in. Also hit occasional lobs.

3. Backcourt play
   a. Recognize the opponent's strengths and weaknesses as soon as possible and play to the weaknesses.
   b. Have a game plan when going into a match but be ready to change it if it is not working.
   c. Keep the opponent back by hitting the ground strokes deep.
   d. Bring the opponent to the net with drop shots only if he/she is poor at volleying or on overheads.
   e. Vary your attack by hitting lobs and low down-the-line and crosscourt shots if the opponent rushes the net.
   f. Use deep crosscourt shots to move the opponent around the court, but do not hit in a pattern.
   g. Be patient when ground stroking from the baseline, but go for winners if your opponent is out of position.

4. All-court play. This term describes play by intermediate and advanced players who are capable of executing most of the shots required to cover the entire court. These players are capable of changing and adjusting their games to meet whatever their opponents are doing.
   a. Have a specific plan in mind when going into a match.
   b. Exploit the opponent's weaknesses and concentrate on them as long as it is successful.
   c. Follow the serve up to the net unless the returns are winners.
   d. Try to outsteady the opponent.
   e. Go to the net on all short shots by the opponent.

f.   Hit the high-percentage shots, as more points are won because of errors by the opponent than by hitting outright winners.

g.   Hit a variety of shots to keep the opponent from grooving the strokes.

h.   Bring a good baseline player up to the net with drop shots.

i.   Keep a good volleyer away from the net by hitting deep shots and lobbing when he/she does get into volley position.

j.   Stay with a winning game and change a losing plan.

DOUBLES STRATEGY

In this section, strategies for beginning doubles (up-and-back pattern) and intermediate or advanced doubles (side-by-side pattern and Australian doubles) are outlined.

Starting Positions (Up and Back and Side by Side)

1. **Server.** Behind the baseline, midway between the center mark and the singles sideline.

2. **Server's partner.** Middle of the service court (beginners and shorter players stand closer to the net).

3. **Receiver.** Approximately one-half meter (one to two feet) from the singles sideline on the right side, on the singles sideline on the left side.

4. **Receiver's partner.** Middle of the service line of the service court on the player's side of the court (Fig. 8.3).

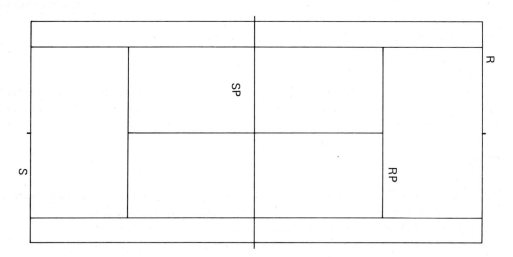

Figure 8.3
Doubles starting positions

Beginning Doubles: Up and Back

The server and receiver play back; their partners play up. Each player is responsible for one-half the court lengthwise, net to baseline. One player protects the right side, and one player protects the left side. The coverage may shift with ball placement. For example, if a ball is lobbed over to the receiver's partner, then the receiver will move to return the ball, and the receiver's partner will shift to the receiver's side of the court.

Strategies

1. Server's strategy
   - ✓ a. Serve to the receiver's backhand.
   - ✓ b. Return all balls in a rally crosscourt, away from the net person.
   - c. Move in to the net or back to the baseline after being pulled in for a short hit. Do not stay in no-man's-land.

2. Server's partner's strategy
   - a. Volley all balls hit within reach.
   - b. Watch the receiver, not the server.
   - ✓ c. Try to make all volleys winners.
   - d. Aim volleys between the receiver and the net person.

3. Receiver's strategy
   - ✓ a. Return all serves and rallies crosscourt, away from the net person.
   - b. Move on in to the net or back to the baseline after being pulled in for a short hit. Do not stay in no-man's-land.

4. Receiver's partner's strategy
   - ✓ a. Move to midservice court as soon as the receiver makes a good crosscourt return or lob past the net person.
   - b. Call serves in or out while standing by the service line.

Intermediate and Advanced Doubles: Side by Side

The server and receiver move to the net beside their partners as quickly as possible. Each player is responsible for one-half the court lengthwise, net to baseline. After the serve and serve reception, partner movement is parallel, with both moving up and back together.

Strategies

1. Server's strategy
   - ✓ a. Come to the net on both serves. Intermediate players who are just learning to approach the net should come in on their first serve and stay back on the second serve.
   - ✓ b. Put more spin on the first serve in order to get the ball in play immediately.
   - ✓ c. Serve wide to slow down an opponent who moves to the net too quickly.
   - ✓ d. Serve to the middle of the court to cut down the angle of return and make it easier for a partner to poach.

2. Server's partner's strategy
   a.   Watch the receiver, not the server. The receiver's movements will telegraph the ball flight.
   b.   Be ready to poach on all balls, particularly those served to the middle of the court.

3. Receiver's strategy
   a.   Return the serve crosscourt, away from the net person.
   b.   Assume that the server will come to the net. Keep the return low to force the server to volley up.
   c.   Come to the net behind the return of serve.
   d.   Lob the return of serve if the server's partner is an effective poacher.

4. Reciever's partner's strategy
   a.   Move to midservice court as soon as the receiver makes a good crosscourt return, a lob, or a pass down the opponent's alley.
   b.   Call serves in or out while standing by the service line.
   c.   Stay midcourt to cut off a return down the middle of the court if the receiver makes a poor return.
   d.   Stand on the baseline if the server's partner is an effective poacher.

Intermediate and Advanced Doubles: Australian Doubles

The server and server's partner are both on the same side of the court. This is a change-of-pace play, usually used on the ad court to force a player with a good backhand crosscourt to hit down the line (Fig. 8.4). For positions and responsibilities on the court, see Side by Side (p. 91).

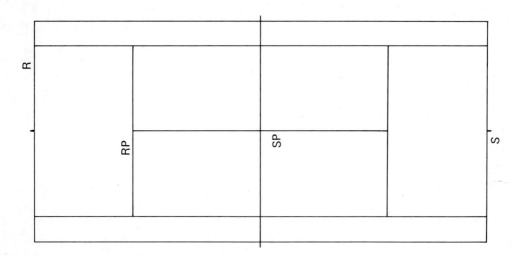

Figure 8.4
Australian doubles position, add side of court

Strategies

1. Server's strategy
   a. Use Australian doubles position on ad court.
   b. Serve wide and move to the right side of the court.

2. Server's partner's strategy
   a. Stand almost at the center of the court in volley position to intercept crosscourt returns.
   b. See strategy for Side by Side (p. 91).

3. Receiver's strategy
   a. Since the server should move to the right side of the court, attempt to lob crosscourt over the net player's head.
   b. Hit fast, low, down-the-line return of service.

4. Receiver's partner's strategy: see Side by Side (p. 91).

SUGGESTED CLASS/STUDENT PROJECTS

1. Have the students observe some tennis matches, looking for strategy by both players or teams.

2. Ask the students to read tennis magazines and books, and to talk with a pro if possible, to add to the strategies already mentioned in class.

3. Have the students prepare specific strategies and attempt to execute them in game situations.

Evaluation

Evaluation, which is generally regarded as a useful means of arriving at a grade for students, should also be applied as an indicator of the skill level of students at different times throughout the course. Tennis instructors should schedule preunit, midunit, and postunit student evaluations, if possible, while making sure that they spend most of their time teaching and not evaluating.

Each instructor must determine whether he/she has time to evaluate the cognitive, psychomotor, and/or affective accomplishments of the students. Instructors must also decide which specific evaluative items will be utilized on these exams.

COGNITIVE EXAMS

The many facets of the cognitive domain can be covered in various ways—lectures, class discussions, demonstrations, student reports, films, film loops, talks and demonstrations by guest professionals, and required readings. Evaluation of student knowledge is most often accomplished either by standardized tests, which often do not meet the course objectives, or by tests devised by individual teachers.

Table 9.1 includes many of the areas from which questions can be selected for the purpose of assessing the student's knowledge of tennis. Instructors should construct their own cognitive exams based on objectives, goals, and class experiences of the students.

For the most part, many of the areas listed in Table 9.1 will be presented at all levels of play. The in-depth presentation will depend on the students' tennis experience and readiness.

PSYCHOMOTOR ASSESSMENT

Tennis instructors must determine whether the evaluation will be objective, subjective, or both. There are standard tests that can be used in tennis-skill testing, but, as in the cognitive area, the psychomotor aspect can be evaluated by appropriate tests constructed by competent teachers.

Table 9.1
Cognitive Assessment Area

	Beginner	Intermediate	Advanced
1. Equipment	X	X	X
2. Facilities	X	X	
3. Rules and safety	X	X	X
4. Scoring			
a. Traditional	X	X	X
b. VASS	X	X	X
c. Tie breakers			
1) 9-point	X	X	X
2) 12-point		X	X
5. Fundamental skills			
a. Ground strokes	X	X	X
b. Volleying	X	X	X
c. Serving	X	X	X
6. Intermediate skills			
a. Slice serve		X	X
b. Lobs		X	X
c. Overheads		X	X
d. Half-volley		X	X
7. Advanced skills			
a. Twist serve			X
b. Chop			X
c. Slice			X
d. Drop shot			X
e. Drop volley			X
8. Strategy			
a. Singles	X	X	X
b. Doubles	X	X	X
9. Terminology	X	X	X

Preunit Psychomotor Assessment

To give a class of beginners a preunit skill test consisting of ground strokes, volleys, and serves could prove to be discouraging. It will only prove what the instructor already knows—that all beginners need help in improving their strokes. Some preunit evaluative techniques, however, are useful to the instructor and will not be too difficult for the students. For example, students could keep the tennis ball in the air by alternating the sides of the tennis racquet while striking the ball.

The test sequence for the above drill would be:

1. The instructor demonstrates while students watch.
   a. Alternate the striking face of the racquet.
   b. Dropped balls are retrieved, and the count is continuous from the last correct hit.
   c. No count is recorded for same side of racquet face hits.

2. Students take a ten-second practice test.

3. Students take a 30-second actual test.

The air dribble using the alternating technique is usually a reliable means of letting the instructors know which students will probably need the most help in learning the basic strokes. Students scoring fewer than 30 alternating hits in a 30-second test usually have the most difficulty in learning to play tennis. Those scoring between 30 and 50 hits might have some difficulties, while those performing more than 50 hits in 30 seconds usually have the fewest problems while learning to ground stroke, volley, and serve.

Ability Grouping

At the first meeting of the class, the instructor can ask the class members to classify themselves as beginners, intermediates, or advanced, and to stand at designated areas on the court. Observation of the students' performance in the various stroke and footwork drills, without balls, will aid in more accurate ability placement.

Midunit Psychomotor Assessment

If time permits, the midunit psychomotor assessment allows the teacher and students to see how much improvement has taken place during the first half of the tennis unit. It should be the same test as that used in the final exam for two very good reasons: (1) it permits students to know what to expect for the final psychomotor test, and (2) it will expedite final testing. In many cases, this will serve as an incentive for the students to practice.

Final Psychomotor Assessment

The final exam should reflect the teacher's expectations about the course objectives for the level of experience of the class. The test should include the strokes that the students have practiced during the unit. The final psychomotor test should be administered approximately one week before the end of the unit to allow for postponements due to inclement weather and student absence. It also allows the instructor to give retakes if deemed necessary.

Psychomotor Assessment of Students with Diverse Skills

Instructors can choose any of various tennis psychomotor tests. Whatever tests are used, such factors as facilities, class time, class size, and the class learning experiences of the students should be considered.

The following tests are suggested because they can be administered easily to large classes with diverse skills and can be adjusted (altering the number of shots attempted) in accordance with facilities and class time.

Ground Stroke Test (Fig. 9.1)

Equipment

One tennis racquet for each student and 20 balls per court.

Court Assignment

1. The tester (T) self-hits the ball from the baseline or midcourt. (A rehit is given if the tester deems that the ground stroker did not have a fair chance to hit the ball.)

2. The ground stroker (GS) stands in ready position approximately one meter (three feet) behind the center mark.

3. The ball height designator stands beside one of the net posts with racquet and arm extended straight up and as high as possible. The height should be kept as constant as possible.

4. The scorer observes and records all attempts and successes—this includes ball height as well as placement.

5. The retriever places the balls at the tester's position and assists the scorer in observation.

If facilities permit, a more accurate ball height designator would be a rope or elastic shock cord stretched approximately 4 meters (12 feet) above the court surface and over the net.

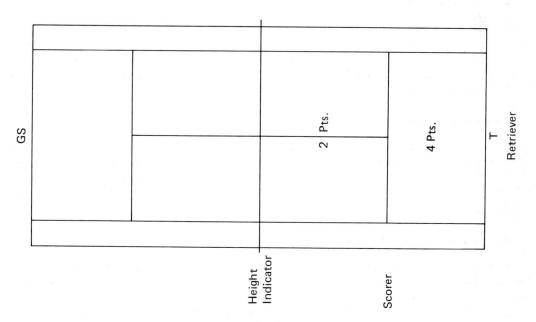

Figure 9.1
Ground stroke test for students with diverse (beginner through advanced) skills

Description

1. The tester drop-hits two practice balls to the forehand and two to the backhand.

2. A total of ten balls will be hit to the student's forehand and backhand. Although the balls should not be hit in any particular order, five balls will be to the forehand side and five to the backhand side.

Scoring

1. Balls hit out of the singles court do not receive any points.

2. Balls hit in the singles court between the net and the service line receive two points.

3. Balls hitting in the singles court between the service line and the baseline receive four points.

4. Balls hitting on the line receive the higher number of points. (See Suggested Standards, p. 101, and Table 9.2).

5. Balls going higher than the ball height designator's reach and landing in the designated court scoring areas will receive one-half the point value for that area. (See Suggested Standards, p. 101, and Table 9.2.)

Volley Test (Fig. 9.2)

Equipment

One racquet for each student and at least 20 balls per court.

Court Assignments

1. The tester (T) self-hits the ball from the baseline. (A rehit is given if the tester deems that the volleyer did not have a fair chance to hit the ball.)

2. The volleyer (V) stands approximately three meters (nine feet) from the net.

3. The scorer observes and records all attempts and successes.

4. The retriever places balls at the tester's position and assists the scorer in observation.

Table 9.2
Suggested Standards for Basic Tennis Skill Tests

Level	Excellent	Good	Fair	Poor
Advanced	87%-100%	73%-86%	59%-72%	45%-58%
Intermediate	73% and above	59%-72%	45%-58%	31%-44%
Beginner	59% and above	45%-58%	31%-44%	17%-30%

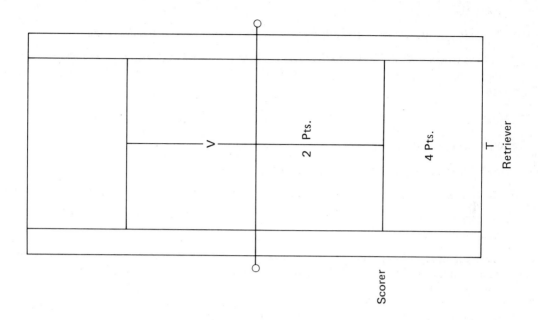

Figure 9.2
Volley test for students with diverse (beginner through advanced) skills

Description

1. The tester drop-hits two practice balls to the forehand and two to the backhand.

2. A total of ten balls will be hit to the student's forehand and backhand. The balls should not be hit in any particular order, but five balls will be to the forehand side and five to the backhand side.

Scoring

1. Balls landing out of the singles court do not receive any points.

2. Balls landing in the singles court between the net and the service line receive two points.

3. Balls landing in the singles court between the service line and the baseline receive four points.

4. Balls landing on the line receive the higher number of points.

Serve Test (Fig. 9.3)

Equipment

One racquet for each student and at least 12 balls per court.

Court Assignments

1. The server (S) stands at singles serving position approximately one meter (one to three feet) to the left or right of the center mark.

2. The scorer observes and records all attempts and successes.

3. The retriever collects balls and assists in observation.

Description

1. Seven balls are placed on each side of the center mark.

2. The server starts from the right side, makes two practice serves, and then five serves to the deuce service court.

3. The server moves to the left side of the center mark and follows the same procedure to the ad service court.

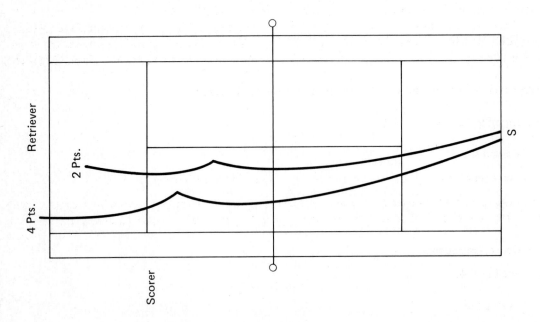

Figure 9.3
Serve test for students with diverse (beginner through advanced) skills

Scoring

1. Balls landing out of the designated service court do not receive any points.

2. Balls landing in the appropriate service courts receive two points when the second bounce is in front of the baseline and four points when the second bounce is on or beyond the baseline.

3. Liners on appropriate service courts are considered good. (See Suggested Standards, below, and Table 9.2.)

Suggested Standards for Basic Tennis Skill Tests

The total possible points on all three tests is 120. To place the students into the appropriate categories, divide the total score each student receives by 120, multiply by 100, and then use Table 9.2.

Scoring the Tennis Skill Tests

Variables that instructors should take into consideration when scoring and rating tennis tests include: the number of weeks (and days per week) that the class meets, the length of each period, and the age level of the students. Because of the possible variables, it is suggested that each teacher establish his/her own local standards.

The objective scores on the three basic stroke tests should not be the only criteria for grading on a tennis unit. All these scores indicate is that the students either can or cannot get the ball across the net and onto the court. The results do not show how well the students stroke the ball. Teachers should subjectively evaluate the stroking abilities of their students (see p. 106).

Sometimes students can register for tennis classes designed exclusively for beginning, intermediate, or advanced players. When this is the case, the basic stroke skill tests mentioned above can be administered to beginners, and the following tests can be given to intermediate and advanced players.

Psychomotor Assessment of Intermediate and Advanced Students

Ground Stroke Test (Fig. 9.4)

Equipment

1. One tennis racquet for each student and a minimum of 20 balls per court.

2. One piece of thin rope (one inch in diameter) long enough to reach from service line to baseline. Tape one end of the rope to the center mark and the other end to the center service line.

Court Assignments

See Fig. 9.4.

Description

1. The tester (T) self-hits two practice hits to the forehand and two to the backhand.

2. The tester should avoid any hitting patterns.

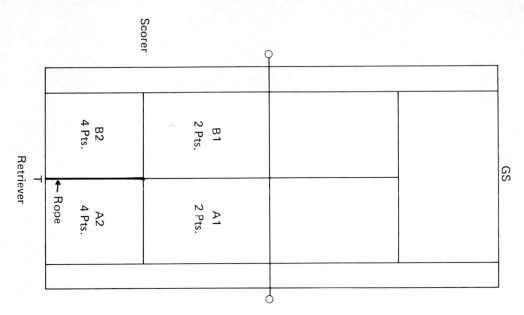

Figure 9.4
Ground stroke test for intermediate and advanced students

3. The ground stroker (GS) hits the first five balls to the back right side of the scoring area (see Fig. 9.4, A2) and the next five balls to the back left side of the scoring area (see Fig. 9.4, B2).

Scoring

1. Balls landing out of the singles court do not receive any points.

2. Balls landing on the designated half of the singles court between the net and the service line receive two points.

3. Balls landing on the designated half of the singles court between the service line and the baseline receive four points.

4. Liners receive the higher number of points.

5. Balls landing in the singles court but not in the designated halves receive one point. (See Suggested Standards, p. 105, and Table 9.2.)

Volley Test (Fig. 9.5)

Equipment

1. One tennis racquet for each student and at least 20 balls per court.

2. One piece of rope long enough to reach from service line to baseline and one inch in diameter. Tape one end of the rope at the center mark and the other end at the center service line.

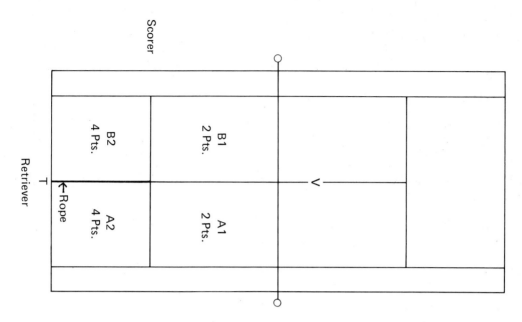

Figure 9.5
Volley test for intermediate and advanced students

Court Assignments

See Fig. 9.5.

Description

1. The tester (T) drop-hits two practice hits to the forehand and two to the backhand.

2. The tester is to avoid any type of hitting pattern.

3. The volleyer (V) hits the first five balls to the back right side of the scoring area (A2) and the next five balls to the back left side of the area (B2).

Scoring

1. Balls landing out of the singles court do not receive points.

2. Balls landing on the designated half of the singles court between the net and service line receive two points.

3. Balls landing on the designated half of the singles court between the service line and baseline receive four points.

4. Liners receive the higher number of points.

5. Balls landing in the singles court but not in the designated halves receive one point. (See Suggested Standards, p. 105, and Table 9.2.)

Serve Test (Fig. 9.6)

Equipment

1. One racquet for each student and at least 16 balls per court.

2. Two pieces of rope, long enough to reach from net to service line and one inch in diameter. Tape one end of each rope at the service line and the other end at the net so as to divide the service courts into two equal courts.

Court Assignments

See Fig. 9.6.

Description

1. Eight balls are placed on each side of the center mark.

2. The server (S) starts from the right side and hits two practice balls.

3. The first three serves for score are hit at the right half of the right service court (A), and the next three are hit at the left half of the right service court (B).

4. The server moves to the left side of the center mark and hits two practice serves to the left service court.

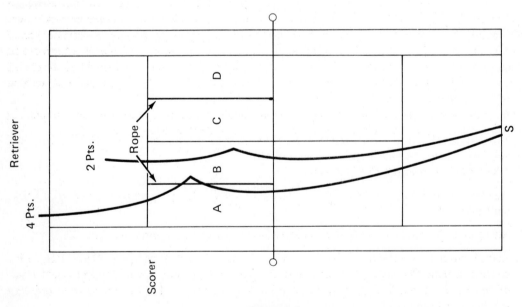

Figure 9.6
Serve test for intermediate and advanced students

5. The first three serves for score are hit at the right half of the left service court (C), and the next three serves are hit at the left half of the left service court (D).

Scoring

1. Balls landing on the designated halves of the service courts receive two points when the second bounce is in front of the baseline and four points if the second bounce is beyond the baseline.

2. Liners on appropriate service court halves are considered good.

3. Serves landing in the appropriate service court but not in the designated halves receive one point. (See Suggested Standards, below, and Table 9.2.)

Suggested Standards for Intermediate and Advanced Tennis Skill Tests

The total possible points on all three tests is 128. To place the students into the appropriate categories, divide the total score of each student by 128, multiply by 100, and use Table 9.2.

Subjective Evaluation

Grades on a tennis unit should not be based solely on an objective test, as it is possible to get a good score on an objective test and at the same time violate some basic principles of a good tennis swing. We therefore suggest that subjective ratings be used in conjunction with objective ratings. Subjective evaluation can be made during any practice or playing time, as well as a scheduled evaluation session. To be most accurate, this type of rating should be used continuously or periodically.

Fig. 9.7 is a tennis subjective analysis chart that can be used to show student progress as well as problem areas. This chart can be used for the duration of the tennis unit. The notations would have more meaning if dates instead of checks were used in the appropriate squares. For example: record the date on which John Doe and Jane Doe were checked on side to the net. John's date would be circled to signify that he did not meet the expected standard, while Jane's date would not be circled because she did it correctly. This system allows instructors to record how long certain students have or have not been making errors.

The items used on the analysis sheet are the more popular concerns of most tennis instructors, but are by no means all-inclusive. The individual instructor can add to, or delete from, the list.

SUGGESTED CLASS/STUDENT PROJECTS

1. Interview at least one tennis instructor and obtain their techniques and tests for evaluating their students.

2. Set up and administer one of the tennis psychomotor tests to three other students.

3. Locate different psychomotor tests for ground strokes, volleys, and serves by reading other tennis instruction books and physical education test and measurement books. Determine which of these are acceptable (e.g., easy to understand, administer, and score) and show satisfactory reliability and validity.

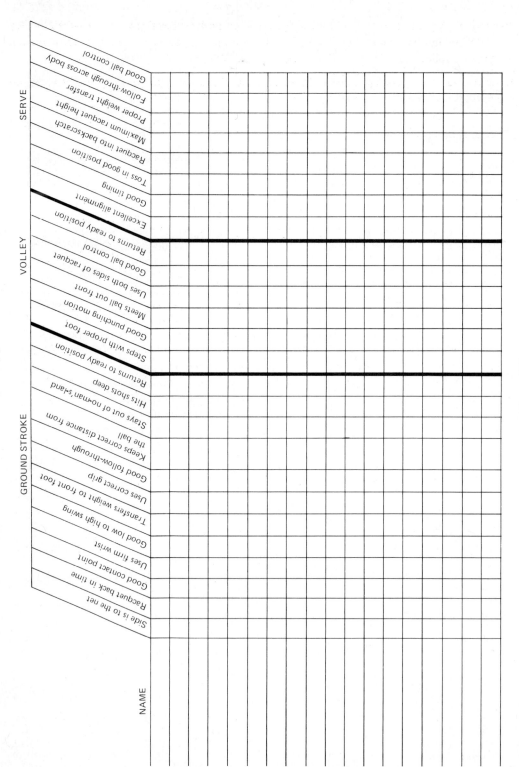

Figure 9.7
Tennis Analysis Sheet

4. Divide the class into groups of five. Have three class members subjectively rate the others as they hit forehand and backhand ground strokes. Compare the judgments of the raters. The same can be done for volleys and serves.

5. Have various class members correct the mistakes as the teacher intentionally makes errors on ground strokes, volleys, and serves.

10

Coaching Tennis

To develop an outstanding tennis program, the coach must be an administrator as well as a teacher. This chapter will discuss the varied duties of a coach by offering suggestions on preseason considerations, team selection, competition, team conditioning, practice session, and coaching.

PRESEASON PLANNING

Schedules

Conference schedules in schools may be completed one to two years in advance by conference scheduling committees. Nonconference games and invitational tournaments should be arranged for the coming year at the end of the current season. Try not to schedule all weak or all strong competition in sequence; schedule no more than two competitions a week. Parent-student and local tennis club-student practice matches are good early season openers, which will increase parental and community support for the program.

Contracts

As soon as the match schedule has been finalized, the home team should send written contracts stating the date, time, and place of the competition to the visiting team for final signature approval.

Budget

The budget submitted by the coach to the athletic director or recreation department will be based primarily on the match schedule, conference fees, and equipment and uniform requirements. Most schools prepare a standard request form for all sports; the line items peculiar to a specific sport are completed by the coach (Fig. 10.1). Balls, team travel, and uniforms are the big yearly expenses for tennis. Each player on the team should have a uniform. For a varsity and junior varsity team, approximately 12 uniforms will be needed. Balls are usually furnished by the home teams. With each individual match played using two balls, and allowing two additional balls for three set matches, 12 cans per school match involving a varsity and junior varsity team would be necessary. Add to this practice

SPORT_____ YEAR _____

COACH_____

	BUDGET	EXPENDED	BALANCE
Scouting			
Meetings and clinics			
Books, periodicals			
Photo services			
Telephone and telegraph			
Dues, memberships			
Uniforms			
Equipment			
1.			
2.			
3.			
Team travel			
Dual meets away			
1.			
2.			
3.			
4.			
5.			
6.			
District meet			
State meet			
Nonbudgeted expenses			
1.			
2.			
TOTAL			

Figure 10.1
Budget

balls for the season, and 24 to 36 dozen balls is a minimum order. Distance and number of away meets will determine the travel budget. Net replacement is not always necessary; it may be included in the physical education budget or shared by the physical education and athletic departments.

Bids

Requests for bids on needed equipment and uniforms should be initiated as soon as the budget is approved by the athletic director. Purchases should be completed during the off-season.

Travel

A school bus or van should be reserved for each of the away matches as soon as the schedule is completed.

TEAM SELECTION PROCEDURE

Announcements

Most high schools and colleges rely on tryouts to complete their teams. Team tryout times must be well publicized by court posters and school bulletins. Unless the budget is large enough to furnish balls for tryouts, be sure to indicate that each player is to bring three new balls, well marked, to the first team meeting.

Meeting

The initial meeting of the coach and those who wish to try out should include:

1. Welcoming and introductions. Briefly review past team records.

2. Collecting player information. Each player present should complete an information sheet listing home address, phone, and tennis experience.

3. Issuing season schedule. A printed season schedule should be given to each student at the meeting. This will enable the student to determine whether study/work/social obligations will allow them time to compete.

4. Discussing player eligibility and team requirements. Conference rules regarding grade point average, course hours, and physical examinations should be stressed at the first meeting. Tennis skills desired should also be noted. For example, in most high schools and recreation clubs, the players participate in either singles or doubles, but not both. In colleges and universities, the traveling team is expected to play both singles and doubles.

Tryouts

For those who wish to try out, a two week tryout period is desirable. If there are a large number of players and few courts, the coach may want the players to play three out of five games with as many players as possible within two or three days. Remember, however, that playing three out of five games is not an indication of staying power or player tenacity. If it is apparent that certain players lose to everyone, the coach may thank them for trying, tell them what they need to do to improve, and ask them to try again next year. For those remaining, ten game pro sets or matches should be played. Returning team members should also be required to play for a team position.

Final Selection

Where players are close in ability, the coach should consider the students' singles and doubles play, court attitude, general athletic ability, previous tournament experience, and year in school. How the student strokes is a consideration in final player selection; some players, however, appear to do everything wrong strokewise and still win!

Player Positions

The coach may rely entirely on ladder position when placing the team in a player order or may use judgment when players are close in ability. Conference rules should be checked to see if a requirement for placing players is stated. Whether the lineup is arranged according to ladder play or subjectively, coaches are expected to place their players on the basis of the players' abilities in both singles and doubles.

COMPETITION

Each school conference, recreation department, and tennis club determines its own procedures for competition. Be sure to check on who provides the balls, default procedures, scoring options permitted, and coaching etiquette during play.

Playing lineups, for both singles and doubles, are to be written down before the match starts. Coaches should exchange the lineups simultaneously so that no last-minute changes can be made by either coach.

CONDITIONING

At the competitive level, tennis is a fast, demanding sport, and if the players are close in ability, the player in the best physical condition will win. Some indicators of poor physical condition are missing strokes and failure to position oneself properly. To prepare the players physically, the coach needs to develop off-season and in-season conditioning programs. These programs should include exercises that develop and improve a tennis player's strength, speed, agility, flexibility, and endurance (both cardiovascular and muscular).

Off-season

During the off-season, the conditioning is usually nonspecific. The athlete may engage in some informal, low-intensity running two days a week, and in weight training or calisthenics two or three days a week, and should participate in other sports as well as tennis. The off-season training is up to each individual.

Preseason

A six-week preseason conditioning program is desirable and possible with sports played during the spring season (see Table 10.1). Be sure to check conference rules for season time limitations.

Table 10.1
Suggested Preseason Conditioning Activities

Activity	Reason	Standard
Easy stretches and jog in place	Warm-up	Ten minutes
Run one mile	Endurance	Within 12 minutes
Hip roll (Fig. 10.2)	Flexibility	20 rolls, onto each side
Arm sprints (Fig. 10.3)	Arm-shoulder power	20 regular arm sprints, one-minute rest, and ten fingertip arm sprints
Bench blasts (Fig. 10.4)	Leg power	Perform as many in one minute as possible (40 to 70)
Sit-ups	Abdominal strength	50 bent-knee sit-ups
Jump rope	Agility, endurance	50 times with both feet, 50 times with right foot, 50 times with left foot, 50 times with alternating feet
Windmill (Fig. 10.5)	Flexibility	20 windmills, ten to each side
Wind sprints	Speed, agility	Run six 40-yard wind sprints with a two-minute rest between

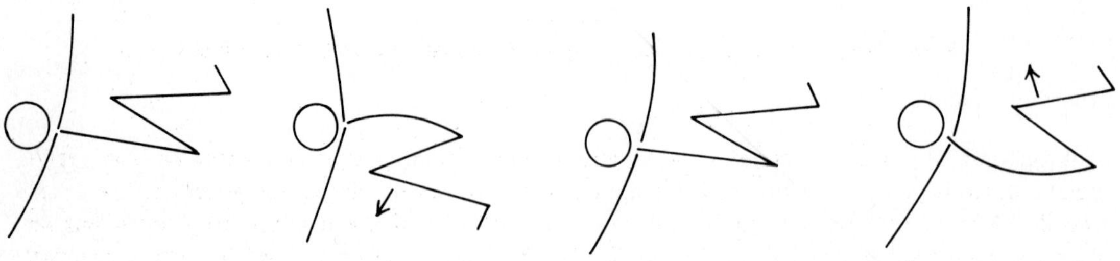

Figure 10.2
Hip roll (bring knees to chest and alternate touching them to floor on right and left)

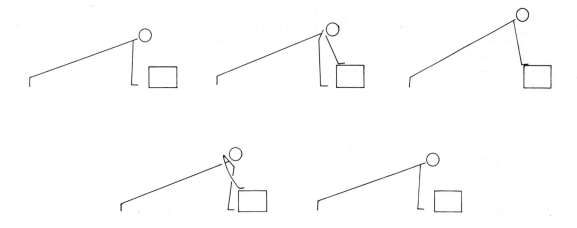

Figure 10.3
Arm sprints (walk up and down stair or box with arms)

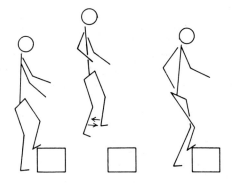

Figure 10.4
Bench blasts (feet alternate touching bench or stair, about 17 inches high)

In general, the preseason conditioning should include three days of intensive running and conditioning drills. If you are meeting with the athletes five days a week during the preseason, the other two days should be spent on tennis strategies and skill drills. Where it is necessary to use indoor facilities, skill practice circuits may be set up. The gymnasium wall space may be used to practice serves and forehand and backhand ground strokes. Continuous volleys using a chair as the net take little space and can be practiced off to the side. Where portable standards and badminton nets are available, a more interesting circuit can be set up. The nets can be arranged for any practice emphasis: serving, ground stroke to volley practice, ground stroke to ground stroke practice, volley to volley practice. Strategies such as coming in behind the serve or poaching can be worked on effectively

Figure 10.5
Windmill (alternate toe touches from standing position)

indoors where nets are available. Last season's tennis balls should be used, since dead tennis balls give just the right bounce on indoor wooden surfaces.

In-season

The in-season conditioning program stresses skill development, scrimmages, challenge matches, and competition more than conditioning. However, some drills should be chosen that improve player skill and physical condition. Examples of skill-conditioning drills follow.

1. **Down-the-line, crosscourt ground stroke sprint drill.** The drill is performed by two players, baseline position, on opposite sides of the court. Player A hits the ball down the singles sideline deep to player B. Player B returns the ball crosscourt deep. Player A sprints to the ball and returns it straight down the singles sideline deep to player B. Player B returns the ball crosscourt deep. Player A sprints to the ball and returns it straight down the singles sideline deep. Player B moves to the ball and returns it crosscourt deep, etc. Players should continue sprinting the width of the court returning well-placed balls until time is called.

2. **Scramble backcourt (Fig. 10.6).**   This drill is performed by two players. Player A is positioned at center court, approximately eight feet from the net, with a large supply of balls. Player B is positioned in the center of the baseline on the opposite side of the net. Player A hits balls first to the right singles sideline, then the left singles sideline, continuously, allowing B just enough time to scramble back to starting position in between hits.
   VARIATION: **Scramble net.** Player A at baseline, player B at net. Same pattern as for scramble backcourt.

3. **Alternate lob-smash.** This drill is performed by two players. Player A is positioned at the baseline with a large supply of balls. Player B stands on the service line on the opposite side of the net, facing player A. Player A lobs short to the service line for a smash return, then deep to the court for a lob return, then short-deep, etc.

4. **Two-step in (Fig. 10.7).** This drill is performed by two players. Players stand directly opposite each other on their own baselines. Player A hits a forehand ground stroke from the baseline to

Figure 10.6
Scramble drill

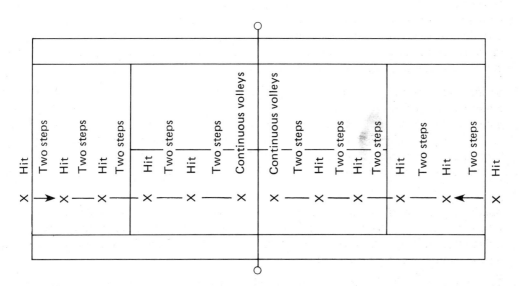

Figure 10.7
Two-step in drill

player B and moves in two steps. Player B returns the ball to player A and moves in two steps. Player A returns the ball from the new court position and moves in two steps, etc., until both players are at volley position at the net. No attempt is made to put the ball away.

On days when less time is spent on skill-conditioning drills and more time on scrimmaging, good conditioning activities to be completed between the first and second sets are: (1) a seven-minute run, (2) six 40-yard sprints, or (3) ten-minute rope jumping. This can be an indicator of the players' performance in a third set as well as a conditioning drill. Even in practices when more time is devoted to drills related to skill conditioning, use at least one conditioning drill suggested for preseason use.

PRACTICE SESSIONS

Practice sessions, including conditioning, should be approximately two hours long, five times a week, including competitive play. Challenge matches may be played over the weekend if the players wish to do so.

Included in the practice sessions will be analysis and correction of player skills, singles and doubles strategies, skill-conditioning drills, and scrimmages. Practices will vary depending on weaknesses observed in the players during practice and competitive events. As an example, if the players are experiencing difficulty on the return of serve, more time may be spent on serve reception practice. The basic format for team practice shown in Table 10.2 may be modified to fit the needs of the players.

COACHING THE PLAYERS

Competitive tennis is a series of singles and doubles matches that result in a team score. Except for doubles, each individual player is responsible for matches won or lost. In conferences where coaching is not permitted once the match begins, the players must make all decisions. This means that the coach must help the players know their own strengths, use them well, and be able to analyze the opponents' weaknesses and play them.

Before the match begins, not only the coach, but also the players need to encourage each other to do their best so that morale will be high and each player will walk on the court with confidence. During the match, the coach and other players on the sideline should applaud good efforts of the team members playing and urge them on with positive hand signals when their play is faltering. At the end of the match, the coach should shake hands with each player, congratulate the winners, comment *favorably* on the good points of the losers' match, and perhaps mention drills to be used at the next practice. Thank each player for their efforts, win or lose.

As a coach, when you are losing, never moan, "Why are my players doing this to me?" It's their match, and chances are they want to win for themselves, the team, and the coach. It is not a personal affront to the coach when they lose. A loss indicates that the coach may need to review practice skill drills, diagnose player skills again, and review strategies. If the coach plans well, is enthusiastic, understands the players, and knows tennis techniques, then team members will perform as well as they are able. As a coach, all you can ask is that the team members play their best against all opponents and always engage in matches with the expectation of a win!

Table 10.2
Suggested Daily Practice Schedule

10 minutes	Stretches. Jog and sprint around the outside of the tennis court complex.
5 minutes	Volley from midservice court, keeping the ball in continuous play. Emphasize stepping to the ball and keeping the racquet in front of the body at all times.
5 minutes	Volley from service line to service line, keeping the ball in continuous play. Emphasis as above.
5 minutes	Crosscourt forehand ground strokes from baseline to baseline. Emphasize consistency, early backswing.
5 minutes	Crosscourt backhand ground strokes from baseline to baseline. Emphasis as above.
10 minutes	Down-the-line, crosscourt forehand, backhand ground stroke sprint (see p. 114).
10 minutes	Lob and smash practice. Direct setups to partner as well as moving drills (p. 114).
10 minutes	Two-step in (see p. 115).
10 minutes	Serve for accuracy. Coach indicates which part of the service court to aim for: inside corner, middle of service court, or alley corner.
10 minutes	Serve and come to the net behind the serve. Both server and receiver come in to the net and attempt to put the ball away at the net.
40 minutes	Game play and/or strategy. Pro sets and VASS could be used in order to increase the number of games played.

SUGGESTED CLASS/STUDENT PROJECTS

1. Complete the preseason and in-season drills outlined in this chapter over a one- to two-week period. Note those drills that you would delete or add drills that you consider better.

2. Assist a local coach in designing team practice procedures for his/her team's particular needs.

3. Visit a local coach and discuss how he/she selects team members and decides on player placement.

4. Attend a tennis match and observe coach/player relationship, player/opponent relationship, and player/teammate relationship. If the behavior of individual players does not conform to tennis etiquette, get the coach's personal reaction. As a result of the observation and interview, write down what you think is the coaching philosophy of each coach.

5. Write your own philosophy of coaching.

Appendix I
*Basic Tennis Rules for Class Handouts**

GAME PROCEDURES

1. The game of tennis can be played officially in the form of singles (one against one) or doubles (two against two). After the serve, it is the object for each player (or doubles team) to hit the ball once each time the ball is stroked to his/her (their) side of the net. Hits must land in the designated boundaries on the opponent's side. Stroking is continued alternately until someone knocks the ball out of bounds or into the net.

2. The first server of a match is determined by the toss of a coin or by the spin of a racquet. If player A spins the racquet, player B guesses whether a designated mark on the racquet will be face up or down upon the completion of the spin. Whoever wins the toss or spin chooses one of the following:
   a. To serve.
   b. To receive.
   c. The side of court from which to start.

   If A chooses to serve, B chooses the side on which to receive. If A chooses to receive, B chooses the side on which to start service. If A chooses the side of the court, B chooses whether to serve or receive.

3. The server will serve the first point from behind the baseline and to the right of the center mark. The second point is served from behind the baseline and to the left of the center mark. The server continues to alternate serving sides at the end of each point until the game is completed. (See VASS system, p. 121.)

4. The server is allowed two attempts to get the ball into the appropriate service court. If neither serve is good, the server loses the point.

5. In singles, the players alternate serving games throughout the match, changing sides of the net on odd-numbered game totals.

* For complete United States Tennis Association Rules, see Appendix II.

6. In doubles, teams alternate serving throughout the match. If A and B are playing C and D, the service sequence will be:

> 1st game—A
> 2nd game—C
> 3rd game—B
> 4th game—D

Once the serving rotation has been established, it must be continued until the end of the set (see section on scoring, pp. 120-123). The rotation may be changed at the start of a new set. The teams change sides of the net on odd-numbered game totals.

ADDITIONAL SIMPLIFIED TENNIS RULES

1. The server must keep either foot from contacting the baseline until the racquet has made contact with the ball. Any violation results in a foot fault, which renders the serve no good.

2. If the server misses the ball in an attempt to serve it, the service is a fault.

3. *Let:* A served ball is called a "let service" when (a) it clips the top of the net and then lands in the proper service court, or (b) it is served before the opponent is ready to receive, or (c) it touches the net, goes over, and touches the receiver before hitting the ground. A let serve does not count, and the server must serve again until a good serve is made, or until he/she has served two faults. The number of lets is unlimited. A ball touching the net in a rally is not a let and is played as if it had not touched the net.

   A let ball can be called in situations other than the serve. For example, if an animal, a ball from another court, or some other object goes into a court during a rally, a let ball is declared and the point is replayed. The server is allowed two attempts on the next serve, even if the let ball occurred on the second serve.

4. The person receiving the serve can stand anywhere he/she wants to, provided the served ball is not hit before it has bounced in the proper service court.

5. The server wins the point if the served ball touches the receiver (or receiver's partner in doubles) before it hits the ground unless it is a let ball.

6. When a legal serve bounces in the proper service court, the ball is in play, and a player will win a point if the opponent:
   a. Allows the ball to bounce more than once, on his/her side of the net, before hitting it.
   b. Strokes the ball out of bounds.
   c. Allows the ball to come in contact with his/her body or clothing.
   d. Allows his/her racquet, body, or clothing to come in contact with the net or post while the ball is in play.
   e. Reaches over the net to volley the ball.
   f. Throws the racquet at the ball.
   g. Is out of bounds and the ball comes in contact with him/her before it bounces. Should the ball contact the player's racquet, while out of bounds, it would be in play if returned in bounds.

  h.   Intentionally distracts the other player.
  i.   Hits the ball more than once before returning it.

7. Balls landing on any part of the boundary line are considered good.

8. In doubles, the order of serving and receiving is decided at the beginning of each set. It cannot be changed during the set, but it can be changed at the start of the next set.

9. When there is an error in the service order, the partner who should have served does so as soon as the mistake is discovered. All points scored or faults committed will stand. If the error is discovered at the end of the game, the game and the service order remain as altered.

10. When there is an error in receiving, the mistake stands until the end of the game. The receiving order is corrected when the team receives again.

SCORING

In recent years, different scoring methods for tennis matches have evolved. The scoring options include traditional scoring, Van Allen Simplified Scoring (VASS), and pro set scoring. For each system, either a nine-point or a twelve-point tie breaker may be used. The options are described below.

Traditional Scoring

1. The units included in traditional scoring are points, games, sets, and match.

2. Game scoring is:

   No score—love
   First point—15
   Second point—30
   Third point—40
   Fourth point—game

3. A player winning the fourth point wins that game, provided the other player has not scored more than two points.

4. When both players have won three points each, the score is 40-40 (or deuce). One of the players must win two consecutive points, after deuce, to win the game. If the server wins the point at deuce, the score becomes ad in (which is short for advantage server). If the receiver wins the next point, the score returns to deuce. When the receiver wins the point at deuce point, the score is ad out (short for advantage receiver). The player who won the advantage point must also win the following point to win the game.

5. **Set scoring.** A set is won when one of the players wins six games and the opponent has not won more than four games. If the set score is 6-5, play continues until one of the players is two games ahead. The exception to this is when the tie breaker is in effect (p. 121).

6. **Match.** Tournament directors predetermine the number of sets that will constitute a match. They work within the rules, which state that the maximum number of sets in a match shall be five or, when women take part, three.

Van Allen Simplified Scoring (VASS)

The Van Allen Simplified Scoring system uses one, two, three, and four as the units for scoring a game. The first player to win four points wins the game. When the game score is at 3-3, the receiver gets the choice of receiving the serve in the deuce or ad service court. As in traditional scoring, one player serves an entire game.

Pro Set Scoring

The pro set is won when one of the players wins eight or ten games and is ahead by two games at the time. Pro sets are usually played in exhibition matches and club matches when time does not permit two out of three sets. When games are tied at 7-7 or 9-9, a tie breaker is used.

Tie Breakers

The tie breaker system has been devised to keep tennis matches from lasting too long. Without a tie breaker, it is possible for a two-out-of-three-set match to end at a score of 10-12, 14-12, 16-14, or even higher! The tie breaker prevents such long sets from occurring. The two types used most frequently are the nine-point tie breaker and the twelve-point tie breaker.

Nine-Point Tie Breaker (Sudden Death) *

Five out of nine points.

At 6 all in games, the player whose turn it is to serve puts the ball into play for the first two points of the tie breaker.

Singles. Player A serves points 1 and 2, right court and left court; player B serves points 3 and 4 (right and left). Players then change sides. Player A serves points 5 and 6 (right and left); player B serves points 7 and 8 (right and left). If the score reaches 4 points all, player B serves point 9. The receiver has the choice of courts in which to receive. The set is recorded as seven games to six.

Players change sides during the tie breaker without rest.

The tie breaker counts as one game in reckoning ball changes.

NOTE: If a ball change is called for on the tie breaker game, the change should be deferred until the second game of the following set, to preserve the alternation of the right to serve first with new balls. The players stay for one game after a tie breaker. Player B serves first in the set following the playing of the tie breaker, thus assuring that he/she will be first server if this set also goes into a tie breaker.

A	R	L			R	L			
B			R	L			R	L	R*-L

Change sides ⟶   *Receiver's choice of court

*Explanation of nine-point and twelve-point tie breakers courtesy of Wilson Sporting Goods Co.

Doubles. (A and B) versus (C and D). Assume that player D has served the twelfth game. The same procedure as in singles will apply, *except* that each player serves from the same end of the court in the tie breaker game that he/she has served from during that particular set. This operates to alter the sequence of serving by the partners on the second team. Player A serves points 1 and 2, right court and left court; player D serves points 3 and 4 (right and left). Teams then change sides. Player B serves points 5 and 6 (right and left); player C serves points 7 and 8 (right and left). If the score reaches 4 points all, player C serves point 9. The receiving team has the choice of courts in which to receive. The set is recorded as seven games to six.

Teams stay for one game after a tie breaker, with team (C and D) to serve first.

A&B	AR	AL			BR	BL			
C&D			DR	DL			CR	CL	C*

Change sides ⟶ *Receiver's choice of court

The Twelve-Point Tie Breaker (Wimbledon Method No. 2)

Seven out of 12 points.

At 6 all in games, the player whose turn it is to serve puts the ball into play for the first point of the tie breaker.

Singles. Player A serves point 1, right court; player B serves points 2 and 3, left court and right court; player A serves points 4 and 5 (left and right); player B serves point 6 (left). Players then change sides. Player B then serves point 7 (right). Player A serves points 8 and 9 (left and right); player B serves points 10 and 11 (left and right); player A serves point 12 (left). If either player wins seven points, by a margin of two points, the set is recorded as seven games to six.

If the score reaches 6 points all, the players then change sides, and players continue to serve as before until one player establishes a margin of two points. Player A serves point 13, right court; player B serves points 14 and 15, left court and right court; player A serves points 16 and 17 (left and right); player B serves point 18 (left). If the score is still tied, the players change sides every six points and repeat this procedure.

Players change sides during the tie breaker without rest.

The tie breaker counts as one game in reckoning ball changes. If a ball change is called for on the tie breaker game, new balls should be used.

The players change sides for one game after a tie breaker. Player B serves first in the set following the playing of the tie breaker, thus assuring that he/she will be first server if this set also goes into a tie breaker.

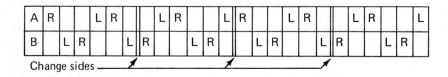

Doubles. (A and B) versus (C and D). Assume that player D has served the twelfth game. The same procedure as in singles will apply. Players preserve the sequence of their serving turns. Player A serves point 1, right court; player C serves points 2 and 3, left court and right court; player B serves points 4 and 5 (left and right); player D serves point 6 (left). Teams then change sides. Player D then serves point 7 (right); player A serves points 8 and 9 (left and right); player C serves points 10 and 11 (left and right); player B serves point 12 (left). If either team wins seven points, by a margin of two points, the set is recorded as seven games to six.

If the score reaches 6 points all, teams change sides, and players continue to serve as before until one team establishes a margin of two points. Player B serves point 13, right court; player D serves points 14 and 15, left court and right court; player A serves points 16 and 17 (left and right); player C serves point 18 (left). If the score is still tied, teams then change sides every six points and repeat this procedure with the continuing sequence of service.

Teams change sides for one game after a tie breaker, with team (C and D) to serve first.

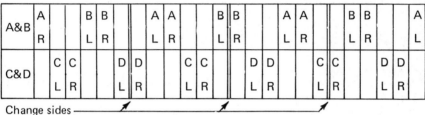

Appendix II
United States
Tennis Association
*Rules of Tennis**

THE SINGLES GAME

Rule 1

Dimensions and Equipment

The court shall be a rectangle 78 feet (23.77m) long and 27 feet (8.23m) wide. It shall be divided across the middle by a net suspended from a cord or metal cable of a maximum diameter of one-third of an inch (0.8cm), the ends of which shall be attached to, or pass over, the tops of two posts, 3 feet 6 inches (1.07m) high, and not more than 6 inches (15cm) in diameter, the centers of which shall be 3 feet (0.91m) outside the court on each side. The net shall be extended fully so that it fills completely the space between the two posts and shall be of sufficiently small mesh to prevent the ball's passing through. The height of the net shall be 3 feet (0.914m) at the center, where it shall be held down taut by a strap not more than 2 inches (5cm) wide and white in color. There shall be a band covering the cord or metal cable and the top of the net for not less than 2 inches (5cm) nor more than 2½ inches (6.3cm) in depth on each side and white in color. There shall be no advertisement on the net, strap, band or singles sticks. The lines bounding the ends and sides of the Court shall respectively be called the Baselines and the Sidelines. On each side of the net, at a distance of 21 feet (6.40m) from it and parallel with it, shall be drawn the Service lines. The space on each side of the net between the service line and the sidelines shall be divided into two equal parts, called the service courts, by the center service line, which must be 2 inches (5cm) in width, drawn half-way between, and parallel with, the sidelines. Each baseline shall be bisected by an imaginary continuation of the center service line to a line 4 inches (10cm) in length and 2 inches (5cm) in width called the center mark, drawn inside the Court at right angles to and in contact with such baselines. All other lines shall be not less than 1 inch (2.5cm) nor more than 2 inches (5cm) in width, except the baseline, which may be 4 inches (10cm) in width, and all measurements shall be made to the outside of the lines.

*Reprinted by permission of the United States Tennis Association Incorporated.

Rule 2

Permanent Fixtures

The permanent fixtures of the Court shall include not only the net, posts, cord or metal cable, strap and band, but also, where there are any such, the back and side stops, the stands, fixed or movable seats and chairs around the Court, and their occupants, all other fixtures around and above the Court, and the Chair Umpire, Net Umpire, Line Umpires and Ball Boys when in their respective places.

Rule 3

Ball—Size, Weight and Bound

The ball shall have a uniform outer surface and shall be white or yellow in color. If there are any seams they shall be stitchless. The ball shall be more than two and a half inches (6.35cm) and less than two and five-eighths inches (6.67cm) in diameter, and more than two ounces (56.7 grams) and less than two and one-sixteenth ounces (58.5 grams) in weight. The ball shall have a bound of more than 53 inches (135cm) and less than 58 inches (147cm) when dropped 100 inches (254cm) upon a concrete base. The ball shall have a forward deformation of more than .220 of an inch (.56cm) and less than .290 of an inch (.74cm) and a return deformation of more than .350 of an inch (.89cm) and less than .425 of an inch (1.08cm) at 18 lbs. (8.165 kg) load. The two deformation figures shall be the averages of three individual readings along three axes of the ball and no two individual readings shall differ by more than .030 of an inch (.08cm) in each case.

Regulations for conducting tests for bound, size and deformation of balls may be found on page 515 of the 1979 USTA Yearbook or obtained from USTA in New York.

Rule 4

The Racket

The racket shall consist of a frame and a stringing. The frame may be of any material, weight, size or shape.

The strings must be alternately interlaced or bonded where they cross, and each string must be connected to the frame. If there are attachments, they must be used only to prevent wear and tear and must not alter the flight of the ball. The density in the center must be at least equal to the average density of the stringing. The stringing must be made so that the moves between the strings will not exceed that which is possible, for instance, with 18 mains and 18 crosses uniformly spaced and interlaced in a stringing area of 75 square inches.

Rule 5

Server and Receiver

The Players shall stand on opposite sides of the net; the player who first delivers the ball shall be called the Server, and the other the Receiver.

Rule 6

Choice of Ends and Service

The choice of ends and the right to be Server or Receiver in the first game shall be decided by toss. The player winning the toss may choose, or require his opponent to choose:

(a)   The right to be Server or Receiver, in which case the other player shall choose the end; or

(b)   The end, in which case the other player shall choose the right to be Server or Receiver.

Note—*These choices should be made promptly, and are irrevocable.*

Rule 7

Delivery of Service

The service shall be delivered in the following manner. Immediately before commencing to serve, the Server shall stand with both feet at rest behind (i.e. farther from the net than) the base-line, and within the imaginary continuations of the center-mark and side-line. The Server shall then project the ball by hand into the air in any direction and before it hits the ground strike it with his racket, and the delivery shall be deemed to have been completed at the moment of the impact of the racket and the ball. A player with the use of only one arm may utilize his racket for the projection.

Rule 8

Foot Fault

The Server shall throughout the delivery of the service:

(a)   Not change his position by walking or running.

(b)   Not touch, with either foot, any area other than that behind the baseline within the imaginary extention of the center-mark and sideline.

EXPLANATION: The service begins when the Server takes a ready position and ends when his racket makes contact with the ball.

Note: The following interpretation of Rule 8 was approved by the Intenational Federation on 9th July, 1958:

(a)   The Server shall not, by slight movements of the feet which do not materially affect the location originally taken up by him, be deemed "to change his position by walking or running."

(b)   The word "foot" means the extremity of the leg below the ankle.

COMMENT: This rule covers the most decisive stroke in the game, and there is no justification for its not being obeyed by players and enforced by officials. No tournament official has the right to request or attempt to instruct any umpires to disregard violations of it.

Rule 9

From Alternate Courts

(a)   In delivering the service, the Server shall stand alternately behind the right and left Courts, beginning from the right in every game. If service from a wrong half of the Court occurs and is undetected, all play resulting from such wrong service or services shall stand, but the inaccuracy of the station shall be corrected immediately it is discovered.

b)   The ball served shall pass over the net and hit the ground within the Service Court which is diagonally opposite, or upon any line bounding such Court, before the Receiver returns it.

COMMENT: The Receiver is not allowed to volley a served ball, i.e., he must allow it to strike in his court first (See Rule 18 (a)).

Rule 10

Faults

The Service is a fault:
(a)   If the Server commits any breach of Rules 7, 8 or 9;
(b)   If he misses the ball in attempting to strike it;
(c)   If the ball served touches a permanent fixture (other than the net, strap or band) before it hits the ground.

Rule 11

Service After a Fault

After a fault (if it be the first fault) the Server shall serve again from behind the same half of the Court from which he served that fault, unless the service was from the wrong half, when, in accordance with Rule 9, the Server shall be entitled to one Service only from behind the other half. A fault may not be claimed after the next service has been delivered.

Rule 12

Receiver Must Be Ready

The Server shall not serve until the Receiver is ready. If the latter attempts to return the service, he shall be deemed ready. If, however, the Receiver signifies that he is not ready, he may not claim a fault because the ball does not hit the ground within the limits for the service.

Note: The Server must wait until the Receiver is ready for the second service as well as the first, and if the Receiver claims to be not ready and does not make any effort to return a service, the Server may not claim the point, even though the service was good.

Rule 13

A Let

Note: A service that touches the net in passing yet falls into the proper court (or touches the receiver) is a let. This word is used also when, because of an interruption while the ball is in play, or for any other reason, a point is to be replayed.

In all cases where a let has to be called under the rules, or to provide for an interruption to play, it shall have the following interpretations:
(a)   When called solely in respect of a service, that one service only shall be replayed.
(b)   When called under any other circumstance, the point shall be replayed.

Note: A spectator's outcry (of "out," "fault" or other) is not a valid basis for replay of a point, but action should be taken to prevent a recurrence.

Rule 14

The Service Is a Let

The service is a let:
(a) If the ball served touches the net, strap or band, and is otherwise good, or, after touching the net, strap or band, touches the Receiver or anything which he wears or carries before hitting the ground.
(b) If a service or a fult is delivered when the Receiver is not ready (see Rule 12).

In case of a let, that particular service shall not count, and the Server shall serve again, but a service let does not annul a precious fault.

COMMENT: Note that a let called on second service because the Receiver was not ready does not annul the first-servive fault. Second service to come.

Rule 15

When Receiver Becomes Server

At the end of the first game the Receiver shall become the server, and the Server Receiver; and so on alternately in all the subsequent games of a match. If a player serves out of turn, the player who ought to have served shall serve as soon as the mistake is discovered, but all points scored before such discovery shall be reckoned. If a game shall have been completed before such discovery, the order of service remains as altered. A fault served before such discovery shall not be reckoned.

Note: If an error in serving sequence occurs and is discovered during a TIE-BREAKER game the serving sequence should be adjusted immediately so as to bring the number of points served by each player into the fairest possible balance. All completed points shall count.

Rule 16

When Players Change Ends

The players shall change ends at the end of the first, third and every subsequent alternate game of each set, and at the end of each set unless the total number of games in such set be even, in which case the change is not made until the end of the first game of the next set.

If a mistake is made and the correct sequence is not followed the players must take up their correct station as soon as the discovery is made and follow their original sequence.

*EXPLANATION: If the mistake is discovered **during** a game the change in ends will be made at once, with all points that have been played counting, and the rest of that game, even if it be only one point, counting as a game. If the mistake is discovered at the **end** of a game, action that involves the smallest number of changes to get back to the original sequence of court occupancy, with an equitable division of games-per-end-per-player, should be taken.*

Rule 17

Ball in Play Till Point Decided

A ball is in play from the moment at which it is delivered in service. Unless a fault or let be called, it remains in play until the point is decided.

COMMENT: A point is not "decided" simply when, or because, a good shot has clearly passed a player, nor when an apparently bad shot passes over a baseline or sideline. An outgoing ball is still definitely "in play" until it actually strikes the ground, backstop or a permanent fixture, or a player. The same applies to a good ball, bounding after it has landed in the proper court. A ball that becomes imbedded in the net is out of play.

Rule 18

Server Wins Point

The Server wins the point:
(a)   If the ball served, not being a let under Rule 14, touches the Receiver or anything which he wears or carries, before it hits the ground;
(b)   If the Receiver otherwise loses the point as provided by Rule 20.

Rule 19

Receiver Wins Point

The Receiver wins the point:
(a)   If the Server serves two consecutive faults;
(b)   If the Server otherwise loses the point as provided by Rule 20.

Rule 20

Player Loses Point

A player loses the point if:
(a)   He fails, before the ball in play has hit the ground twice consecutively, to return it directly over the net (except as provided in Rule 24 (a) or (c)); or
(b)   He returns the ball in play so that it hits the ground, a permanent fixture, or other object, outside any of the lines which bound his opponent's Court (except as provided in Rule 24 (a) and (c)); or
(c)   He volleys the ball and fails to make a good return even when standing outside the Court; or
(d)   **In playing the ball he deliberately carries or catches it on his racket or deliberatley touches it with his racket more than once; or**
EXPLANATION: Only when there is a definite "second push" by the player does his shot become illegal, with consequent loss of point. (See Tournament Regulation 16).
(e)   He or his racket (in his hand or otherwise) or anything which he wears or carries touches the net, post (single stick, if they are in use), cord or metal cable, strap or band, or the ground within his opponent's Court at any time while the ball is in play (touching a pipe

support running across the court at the bottom of the net is interpreted as touching the net); [See Note at Rule 23] ; or

(f)   He volleys the ball before it has passed the net; or

(g)   The ball in play touches him or anything that he wears or carries, except his racket in his hand or hands; or

Note: *that this loss of point occurs regardless of whether the player is inside or outside the bounds of his court when the ball touches him. A player is considered to be "wearing or carrying" anything that he was wearing or carrying at the beginning of the point during which the touch occurred.*

(h)   He throws his racket at and hits the ball.

EXAMPLE: Player has let racket go out of his hand clearly before racket hits ball, but the ball rebounds from his racket into proper court. This is not a good return; player loses point.

Rule 21

Player Hinders Opponent

If a player commits any act which hinders his opponent in making a stroke, then, if this is deliberate, he shall lose the point or if involuntary, the point shall be replayed.

Rule 22

Ball Falling on Line—Good

A ball falling on a line is regarded as falling in the Court bounded by that line.

COMMENT: In matches played without officials, it is customary for each player to make the calls on all balls hit to his side of the net, and if a player cannot call a ball out with surety he should regard it as good.

Rule 23

Ball Touching Permanent Fixture

If the ball in play touches a permanent fixture (other than the net, posts, cord or metal cable, strap or band) after it has hit the ground, the player who struck it wins the point; if before it hits the ground his opponent wins the point.

Rule 24

Good Return

It is a good return:

(a)   If the ball touches the net, post (singles stick, if they are in use), cord or metal cable, strap or band, provided that it passes over any of them and hits the ground within the Court; or

(b)   If the ball, served or returned, hits the ground within the proper Court and rebounds or is blown back over the net, and the player whose turn it is to strike reaches over the net and plays the ball, provided that neither he nor any part of his clothes or racket touch the net, post (singles stick), cord or metal cable, strap or band or the ground within his opponent's Court, and that the stroke is otherwise good; or

(c)   If the ball is returned outside the post or singles stick, either above or below the level of the top of the net, even though it touches the post or singles stick, provided that it hits the ground within the proper Court; or

(d)   If a player's racket passes over the net after he has returned the ball, provided the ball passes the net before being played and is properly returned; or

(e)   If a player succeeds in returning the ball, served or in play, which strikes a ball lying in the Court [i.e. on his court when the point started] .

Note: If, for the sake of convenience, a doubles court is equipped with singles posts for the purpose of a singles game, then the doubles posts and those portions of the net, cord or metal cable and band outside such singles posts shall be regarded as "permanent fixtures *other than* net, post, strap or band," and therefore *not* posts or parts of the net of that singles game.

A return that passes under the net cord between the singles stick and adjacent doubles post without touching either net cord, net or doubles post and falls within the area of play is a good return. (But in doubles this would be a "through"—loss of point.)

Rule 25

Interference

In case a player is hindered in making a stroke by anything not within his control except a permanent fixture of the Court, or except as provided for in Rule 21, the point shall be replayed.

Rule 26

The Game

If a player wins his first point, the score is called *15* for that player; on winning his second point, the score is called *30* for that player; on winning his third point, the score is called *40* for that player, and the fourth point won by a player is scored *game* for that player except as below:

If both players have won three points, the score is called *deuce*; and the next point won by a player is called *advantage for that player*. If the same player wins the next point, he wins the game; if the other player wins the next point the score is again called *deuce;* and so on until a player wins the two points immediately following the score at deuce, when the game is scored for that player.

COMMENT: In matches played without an umpire the Server should announce, in a voice audible to his opponent and spectators, the set score at the beginning of each game, and (audible at least to his opponent) point scores as the game goes on. Misunderstandings will be averted if this practice is followed.

Rule 27

The Set

A player (or players) who first wins six games wins a set; except that he must win by a margin of two games over his opponent and where necessary a set shall be extended until this margin be achieved.

Rule 28

Maximum Number of Sets

The maximum number of sets in a match shall be 5, or, where women take part, 3.

Rule 29

Rules Apply to Both Sexes

Except where otherwise stated, every reference in these Rules to the masculine includes the feminine gender.

Rule 30

Decisions of Umpire and Referee

In matches where a Chair Umpire is appointed his decision shall be final; but where a Referee is appointed an appeal shall lie to him from the decision of a Chair Umpire on a question of law, and in all such cases the decision of the Referee shall be final.

In matches where assistants to the Chair Umpire are appointed (Line Umpires, Net Umpire, Foot-fault Judge) their decisions shall be final on questions of fact, **except that if, in the opinion of the Chair Umpire, a clear mistake has been made, he shall have the right to change the decision of an assistant or order a let to be played.**

When such an assistant is unable to give a decision he shall indicate this immediately to the Chair Umpire who shall give a decision. When the Chair is unable to give a decision on a question of fact he shall order a let to be played.

In Davis Cup or other team matches where a Referee is on court, any decision can be changed by the Referee, who may also instruct the Chair Umpire to order a let to be played.

The Referee, in his discretion, may at any time postpone a match on account of darkness or the condition of the ground or the weather. In any case of postponement the previous score and previous occupancy of courts shall hold good, unless the Referee and the players unanimously agree otherwise.

Rule 31

Play shall be continuous from the first service till the match is concluded:

(a)   Notwithstanding the above, after the third set, or when women take part the second set, either player is entitled to a rest, which shall not exceed 10 minutes, or, in countries situated between Latitude 15 degrees north and Latitude 15 degrees south, 45 minutes, and further-more when necessitated by circumstances not within the control of the players the Chair Umpire may suspend play for such a period as he may consider necessary.

If play is suspended and not resumed until a later day the rest may be taken only after the third set (or when women take part the second set) of play on such later day, completion of an unfinished set being counted as one set.

If play is suspended and not resumed until 10 minutes have elapsed in the same day, the rest may be taken only after three consecutive sets have been played without interruption (or when women take part two sets), completion of an unfinished set being counted as one set.

Any nation is at liberty to modify this provision or omit it from its regulations governing tournaments, matches or competitions held in its own country, other than the international Tennis Championships (Davis Cup and Federation Cup).

(b)   Play shall never be suspended, delayed or interfered with for the purpose of enabling a player to recover his strength or his breath.

(c)   **A maximum of 30 seconds shall elapse from the end of one point to the time the ball is served for the next point, except that when changing ends a maximum of one minute 30 seconds shall elapse from the last point of one game to the time when the ball is served for the first point of the next game.**

These provisions shall be strictly construed. The Chair Umpire shall be the sole judge of any suspension, delay or interference and after giving due warning he may disqualify the offender.

Note: A tournament committee has discretion to decide the time allowed for a warmup period prior to a match. It is recommended that this not exceed five minutes.

USTA Rules Regarding Rest Periods in Age-Limited Categories:

Regular MEN's and WOMEN's, and MEN's 21 and WOMEN's 21—Paragraph A of Rule 31 applies, except that a tournament using tie-breakers may eliminate rest periods provided advance notice is given.

BOYS' 18—All matches in this division shall be best of three sets with NO REST PERIOD, except that in interscholastic, state, sectional and national championships the FINAL ROUND may be best-of-five. If such a final requires more than three sets to decide it, a rest of 10 minutes after the third set is mandatory. Special Note: In severe temperature-humidity conditions a Referee may rule that a 10-minute rest may be taken in Boys' 18 best-of-three. However, to be valid this must be done before the match is started, and as a matter of the Referee's independent judgment.

BOYS' 16, 14 and 12, and GIRLS' 18, 16, 14 and 12—All matches in these categories shall be best of three sets. A 10-minute rest before the third set is MANDATORY in Girls' 12, 14 and 16, and BOYS' 12 and 14. The rest period is OPTIONAL in GIRLS' 18 and BOYS' 16. (Optional means at the option of any competitor.)

All SENIOR divisions (35's, 40's, 45's, 50's and up), and Father-and-Son; Under conventional scoring, all matches best-of-three, with rest period optional.

When 'NO-AD' scoring is used in a tournament . . . A tournament committee may stipulate that there will be no rest periods, even in some age divisions where rest periods would be optional under conventional scoring. These divisions are: regular Men's (best-of-five) and Women's . . . Men's 21 (best-of-five) and Women's 21 . . . Men's 35 . . . Seniors (men 45 and over) . . . Father-and-Son.

N.B. Two conditions of this stipulation are: (1) Advance notice must be given on entry blanks for the event, and (2) The Referee is empowered to reinstate the normal rest periods for matches played under unusually severe temperature-humidity conditions; to be valid, such reinstatement must be announced before a given match or series of matches is started, and be a matter of the Referee's independent judgment.

Rule 32

Coaching

During a match a player may not receive any coaching or advice, except that when a player changes ends he may receive instruction from a Captain who is sitting on the Court in a team competition.

Note: A coach or adviser who disregards the instruction of an umpire or referee to desist from coaching activity at a match will be liable–under USTA Tournament Regulation 9 (a)–to disciplinary action which may include disqualification of the player or removal of the coach or adviser from the court area.

Rule 33

Ball Change Error

In cases where balls are changed after an agreed number of games, if the balls are not changed in the correct sequence the mistake shall be corrected when the player, or pair in the case of doubles, who should have served with the new balls is next due to serve.

THE DOUBLES GAME

Rule 34

The above Rules shall apply to the Doubles Game except as below.

Rule 35

Dimensions of Court

For the Doubles Game the Court shall be 36 feet (10.97m) in width, i.e. 4½ feet (1.37m) wider on each side than the Court for the Singles Game, and those portions of the singles sidelines which lie between the two service lines shall be called the service sidelines. In other respects, the Court shall be similar to that described in Rule 1, but the portions of the singles sidelines between the baseline and the service line on each side of the net may be omitted if desired.

Rule 36

Order of Service

The order of serving shall be decided at the beginning of each set as follows:

The pair who have to serve in the first game of each set shall decide which partner shall do so and the opposing pair shall decide similarly for the second game. The partner of the player who served in the first game shall serve in the third; the partner of the player who served in the second game shall serve in the fourth, and so on in the same order in all subsequent games of a set.

EXPLANATION: It is not required that the order of service, as between partners, carry over from one set to the next. Each team is allowed to decide which partner shall serve first for it, in each set. This same option applies with respect to the order of receiving service.

Rule 37

Order of Receiving

The order of receiving the service shall be decided at the beginning of each set as follows:

The pair who have to receive the service in the first game shall decide which partner shall receive the first service, and that partner shall continue to receive the first service in every odd game, throughout the set. The opposing pair shall likewise decide which partner shall receive the first service in the second game and that partner shall continue to receive the first service in every even game throughout that set. Partners shall receive the service atlernately throughout each game.

EXPLANATION: The receiving formation of a doubles team may not be changed during a set; only at the start of a new set. Partners must receive throughout each set on the same sides of the court which they originally selected when the set began. The first Server is not required to receive in the right court; he may select either side, but must hold this to the end of the set.

Rule 38

Service Out of Turn

If a partner serves out of his turn, the partner who ought to have served shall serve as soon as the mistake is discovered, but all points scored, and any faults served before such discovery shall be reckoned. If a game shall have been completed before such discovery the order of service remains as altered.

Rule 39

Error in Order of Receiving

If during a game the order of receiving the service is changed by the receivers it shall remain as altered until the end of the game in which the mistake is discovered, but the partners shall resume their original order of receiving in the next game of that set in which they are receivers of the service.

Rule 40

Ball Touching Server's Partner Is Fault

The service is a fault as provided for by Rule 10, or if the ball served touch the Server's partner or anything he wears or carries; but if the ball served touch the partner of the Receiver or anything which he wears or carries, not being a let under Rule 14 (a) before it hits the ground, the Server wins the point.

Rule 41

Ball Struck Alternately

The ball shall be struck alternately by one or other player of the opposing pairs, and if a player touches the ball in play with his racket in contravention of this Rule, his opponents win the point.

EXPLANATION: This means that, in the course of making one return, only one member of a doubles team may hit the ball. If both of them hit the ball, either simultaneously or consecutively, it is an illegal return. The partners themselves do not have to "alternate" in making returns. (Mere clashing of rackets does not make a return illegal, if it is clear that only one racket touched the ball.)

Should any point arise upon which you find it difficult to give a decision or on which you are in doubt as to the proper ruling, immediately write, giving full details, to John Stahr, U.S.T.A. Rules Interpretation Committee, 65 Briarcliff Rd., Larchmont, N.Y. 10538, and full instructions and explanations will be sent to you.

Glossary

This tennis glossary has been arranged alphabetically within the categories of scoring, types of shots, parts of a court, rules, strategy, and miscellaneous.

SCORING

Ad   An abbreviation for "advantage." This refers to the point immediately after deuce.

Ad in   The score when the server wins the point immediately after deuce.

Ad out   The score when the receiver wins the point immediately after deuce.

All   Used in reference to tie scores, such as 5 all in the set score (each player has won five games) or 15 all in the game score (each players has won one point in that game).

Deuce   Used when the score is tied at 40-40, and any time it is tied thereafter.

Fifteen   The first point of a game won by the same person or team, if using traditional scoring. (Sometimes, five is used for the first point, but this is erroneous.)

Forty   The third point, won by the same person or team, in a game where traditional scoring is used.

Game   A unit of a set. In traditional scoring a game is won when a player, or team, wins four points without the opponents' winning more than two points. When the scores are tied at 30-30 or 40-40 (deuce), one side must win two consecutive points to win that game. For alternative scoring, see VASS, p. 121.

Game point   A point that could decide the winner of a game.

Love   Tennis score of zero.

Love game   The loser of the game did not win any points.

Love set   The loser of the set did not win any games.

Match   An official tennis match is played between two or among four players. One side usually has to win two sets (out of three) or three (out of five) to win the contest.

Match point   A point that could decide the winner of the match.

No add scoring   An alternative scoring system that gives each point a value of one. The first player to win four points wins the game. (Also called the **VASS** system.)

Pro set   This is a one-set match; the winner is the first side to win eight games and be two games ahead at that time.

Set   A unit of a match. A set is won when a player, or team, wins six games and is two games ahead at that time. When the set score is tied at 5-5, one side must win two consecutive games to win that set (unless the tie breaker is in effect).

Set point   A point that could decide the winner of the set.

Split sets   When each player has won one set and the third set will decide the winner of the match.

Straight sets   When the winner of the match won all the sets played.

Thirty   The second point, won by the same person or team, in a game in which traditional scoring is used.

Tie breaker   A scoring system used to determine the winner of a set when players are tied at 6-6. The nine- and twelve-point tie breakers are used most often. Whoever wins five points first wins the nine-pointer, and whoever gets to seven points first and is ahead by two points wins the twelve-point tie breaker.

VASS   An abbreviation for the Van Allen Simplified Scoring system, also called the "no add" scoring system. See p. 121.

TYPES OF SHOTS

Ace   A winning serve hit beyond the receiver's reach.

American twist   A type of serve that has a combination of top spin and side spin. For a right-handed server, the ball will bounce to the right and high.

Angle volley   A volley that is hit sharply crosscourt.

Approach shot   A shot hit by a player just prior to moving into the volley position.

Backspin shot   A shot with underspin on the ball caused by a forward and downward swing.

Block   A volley or ground stroke executed with little backswing and follow-through.

Cannonball serve   A hard-hit, flat serve.

Chip   A ground stroke, with backspin, that just clears the net.

Crosscourt lob   A ball hit diagonally across the court.

Defensive lob   A shot with a high trajectory, used to recover from poor court position and/or to get the opponent away from the net.

Dink   A softly hit, short shot that is usually not intended to be an outright winner.

Down-the-line shot   A shot hit with the forehand or backhand whose flight travels parallel and close to the sideline on the side of the court from which it was hit.

Drive   A full, forceful shot hit with the forehand or backhand that can force the opponent out of position or be an outright winning shot.

Drop shot   A short ground stroke softly hit, with backspin, that barely clears the net. It is designed to be a winning shot and/or to bring the opponent to the net.

Drop volley   A volley, usually hit with underspin, that just clears the net.

Flat hit   A shot hit with little or no spin.

Ground stroke   A shot made with a full forehand or backhand swing after the ball has bounced.

Half-volley   A defensive shot hit immediately after the ball bounces near the receiver's feet, using little or no backswing.

Kill   A hard-hit overhead or volley usually placed out of the opponent's reach.

Overhead   A servelike motion used to hit a ball that is over the head. Sometimes called a "smash."

Passing shot   A good shot hit out of the reach, on either side, of an opponent in the forecourt.

Serve   The stroke that puts the ball in play to start each point.

Shot hit on the rise   A shot hit after the ball has bounced and before it reaches its peak.

Slice serve   A serve with side spin. It will curve from right to left for a right-hander and from left to right for a left-hander.

Volley   A short backswing and punch shot used to stroke the ball before it bounces, usually used in the forecourt.

PARTS OF A COURT

Ad court   The service court where the server hits the ball when the score is ad in or ad out. (It is the receiver's left service court.)

Alley   A 4½-foot lane on both sides of the singles court, which is used when playing doubles.

Backcourt   The area between the service line and the baseline on either side of the net.

Baseline   The line farthest from the net on each end of the court.

Center mark   A short perpendicular line that denotes the baseline's midpoint.

Center service line   The inside line of all four service courts.

Deuce court   The service court to which the ball is served when the score is deuce. (It is the receiver's right service court.)

Forecourt   The area between the net and the service line on both sides of the net.

No-man's-land   The area between the volley position and the baseline.

Service line   The back line of the service court, parallel to the net.

Sideline   The side boundary of the singles or doubles court. The inside line of the alley is the singles sideline, while the outside line of the alley is the doubles sideline.

RULES

Doubles match   A match played between two teams with two players on each team.

Double fault   A loss of point by the server when both the first and second serves are not hit into the appropriate service court.

Fault   A served ball that does not go into the appropriate service court.

Foot fault   A serving fault caused when the server's foot comes in contact with the court before the racquet contacts the ball, or when the server's foot is on the wrong side of the center mark or appropriate sideline during the service.

Game   A unit of a set. A game is won when a player, or team, wins four points without the opponents' winning more than two points. When the scores are tied at 30-30 or 40-40 (deuce), one side must win two consecutive points to win that game. For alternative scoring, see **VASS**, p. 121.

Let   A term used when a point should be replayed. It happens most often when a serve hits the top of the net and lands in the appropriate service court. (Erroneously called "net serve.")

Long   A term used to indicate that a shot has landed past the baseline.

Mixed doubles   A doubles team consisting of a male and a female as partners.

Out   A term used to indicate that a shot has landed out of bounds.

Singles match   A match played by two players.

STRATEGY

Australian doubles   A formation in which the server and server's partner stand on the same side of the court to start a point.

Baseline game   The style of play for players who prefer to hit ground strokes from the baseline rather than moving to the net.

Change of pace   Changing the speed of the ball by hitting it harder or easier.

Net game   The part of a person's game that involves volleying and overheads.

Pace   Refers to the speed of the ball on various shots.

Poach   Doubles strategy according to which a net person moves to the partner's side of the court to volley a ball intended for the partner.

MISCELLANEOUS

Backswing   The initial part of a tennis stroke that gets the racquet to the back position of the swing.

Break   When a game is won by the receiving player. Also referred to as a "service break."

Break point   When the receiving player needs one point to win the game.

Fast court   Court with a smooth surface, such as cement or grass, which causes the ball to take a hurried (quick) bounce.

Follow-through   The finish of any tennis stroke.

Hacker   A tennis player who is poorly skilled.

Holding serve   When the server wins the game(s).

Rally   A prolonged exchange of shots after the serve.

Slow court   Court with an abrasive surface, which causes the balls to take higher bounces, thus causing a slower game.

References

Bairstow, J. "How to Buy a Racquet." *Tennis* (December 1978), p. 54.

Braden, V., and Bruns, B. *Vic Braden's Tennis for the Future.* Boston: Little, Brown and Co., 1977.

Bright, J. "Your Own Backyard Court: How to Make a Fantasy Come True!" *Tennis* (May 1980), pp. 40-45.

Cox, R. *Teaching Volleyball.* Minneapolis, Minnesota: Burgess Publishing Company, 1980.

Cubbedge, R. "How to Take Care of Your Racquet." *Tennis* (December 1978), pp. 72-73.

Duggan, M. *The Tennis Catalog.* New York: Macmillan Publishing Co. (Rutledge), 1978.

Fox, E., and Mathews, D. *Interval Training.* Philadelphia: W. B. Saunders Co., 1974.

Gould, K. *Tennis, Anyone?* Palo Alto, California: National Press Books, 1971.

Johnson, J. D., and Xanthos, P. J. *Tennis.* Dubuque, Iowa: Wm. C. Brown Co., 1981.

Kennedy, R. "Bigger Is Better." *Sports Illustrated* (September 29, 1980), pp. 62-72.

Lamarche, R. J. "How to Get Your Racquet Strung." *Tennis* (December 1978), pp. 70-71.

——————. and De Jongh, P. "Are Expensive Tennis Shoes Worth It?" *Tennis* (October 1978), pp. 78-83.

Laver, R., and Collins, B., eds. *Tennis Digest.* Northfield, Illinois: Digest Books, 1975.

Leonard, T. "Is One of These New Midsized Racquets the Answer for You?" *Tennis* (August 1979), pp. 40-44.

——————. "Will These New Shapes Help Shape Up Your Game?" *Tennis* (July 1980), pp. 78-83.

——————. "What the Pros Look For in Racquets." *Tennis* (December 1980), pp. 80-84.

Mager, R. F. *Preparing Instructional Objectives.* Belmont, California: Fearon Publishers, 1962.

Murphy, C., and Murphy, B. *Tennis for the Player, Teacher and Coach.* Philadelphia: W. B. Saunders Co., 1975.

Tennis Magazine, eds. *Tennis Strokes and Strategies.* New York: Simon and Schuster, 1975.

Whiddon, S., and Hall, L. *Teaching Softball.* Minneapolis, Minnesota: Burgess Publishing Co., 1980.

Index